FOREWORD

Praise and Worship Songbook Fifteen includes all of the songs from the following Hosanna! Music albums:

Extravagant Grace
Marvelous Things
Rain Down
Rock Of Refuge
We Offer Praises
Your Kingdom Come

Every song is arranged with vocal parts corresponding to the recording, which can easily be performed by your choir or worship team. The piano parts have been simplified from the recording, but follow the basic arrangement.

Musicians should be encouraged to embellish these arrangements by improvising with the chord symbols. When there is a note under a slash (e.g., F/G), the note above the slash is the chord to be played by the upper register instruments (guitar, right hand of the piano, etc.). The note below the slash is to be played by the lower register instruments (bass guitar, organ pedals, left hand of the piano, etc.). For songs that flow smoothly with each other, a medley reference is listed on each appropriate page.

This songbook has many features to help you plan your worship services.

Index "A" lists all songs by key and tempo. Praise and worship times will flow more smoothly if you select songs that are closely related in key and tempo. Create medleys of songs rather than stopping after each song. Choose songs that are related thematically, such as:

Above All	F Major
Grace, Greater Than Our Sin	F Major
My Savior's Love	F Major

Index "B" lists the songs by topic, such as joy, thanksgiving, victory, etc. If you know the theme of your pastor's message, you can prepare the hearts of the people by focusing your worship on the same topic.

Index "C" lists songs by the first line of lyrics in case you are unsure of the title.

Index "D" lists the songs according to their Scriptural references. If you are searching for a song featuring a specific Scripture, you will find it listed in Biblical order.

Index "E" lists copyright owners of the songs presented in this publication.

We wish to thank all those who have given their permission to print the songs in this book. Every effort has been made to locate the copyright owners. If any omissions have occurred, we will make proper corrections in future printings.

TABLE OF CONTENTS

SONG TITLE FROM THE ALBUM

1195

For thou, Lord, art high above all the earth: thou art exalted far above all gods. Psalm 97:9 (NKJV)

Above All

Words and Music by
LENNY LeBLANC
and PAUL BALOCHE

A-bove all wis-dom and all the ways of man,
Ooo.
F
B♭/F
C/E
Dm
Fmaj7/C
You were here be-fore the world be-gan.
B♭
F/A
Gm7
B♭/F
11
A-bove all king-doms, a-bove all
A-bove all king-doms,
C/E
F
F/A
C/B♭
B♭
C

thrones, a-bove all won - ders the world has ev - er known;
a-bove all won - ders;
F Bb/F F F/A C/Bb Bb C
15
A-bove all wealth and treas - ures of the earth,
Ooo.
F Bb/F C/E Dm Fmaj7/C
there's no way to meas - ure what You're worth.
Bb F/A Gm7 Bb/F Asus/E A

20
CHORUS
Parts
Cru - ci-fied, laid be-hind the stone; You
F Gm7 C/E F
lived to die, re - jec-ted and a-lone; Like a rose,
Gm7 C/E F C/E
24
tram-pled on the ground, You took the fall,
Few Voices
Ooo.
Dm Fmaj7/C B♭ F/A

All
1
and thought of me, a-bove all.
Gm7 F/A Bb2 C F
29
2 D.S. 3
all. all. Like a rose,
Bb Csus C F Gm7 C/E F C/E
32
tram-pled on the ground, You took the fall,
Few Voices
Ooo.
Dm Fmaj7/C Bb F/A

Medley Options: I Look to You; Thank You for the Cross.

Oh come, let us worship and bow down; Let us kneel before the Lord our Maker. Psalm 95:6 (NKJ)

Adonai

Words and Music by
CRAIG SMITH

13
our Lord our God,
we bow down,
our Lord our God,
Oo,
E5
D2
we wor - ship,
our Lord, our God.
our Lord, our God.
A2
E5
2, 3.
E5

18
CHORUS
W.L.
A - do - nai,
E - lo - him,
God Most High;
Praise Team
Ah;
God Most High;
C2
D2
E5
22
A - do - nai,
E - lo - him,
Ah;
C2
D2
last time to Coda
1.
God Most High.
God Most High.
E5

2.
D.S. al Coda
E5
Coda
30
Oh, A - do - nai, E - lo - him,
Ah;
E5
C2/E
D2/E
34
God Most High.
God Most High;
E5

Medley options: Draw Me Closer; Holy, Holy, Holy (SCHOLTES).

I will be glad and rejoice in you; I will sing praise to your name, O Most High. Psalm 9:2 (NIV)

All Of Our Praise

Words and Music by
MARK CONDON

we lift You up; You're wor - thy, wor - thy of our praise;
F
B♭maj7
Am7
Gm7 Am7 B♭maj7 C
13
We lift You up,
we lift You up;
F
B♭/C
F
CHORUS 1
17
W.L. ad libs
Lord, You're wor - thy of all of our praise.
We lift You up,
B♭13
A13
A♭13
G13
B♭/C
F
B♭/C
F
B♭/C
we lift You up; You're wor - thy, wor - thy of our praise;
F
B♭maj7
Am7
Gm7 Am7 B♭maj7 C

21
We lift You up, we lift You up; Lord, You're wor - thy of
F Bb/C F Bb13 A13 Ab13 G13
25 CHORUS 2
all of our praise. We clap our hands, we dance and shout; You're wor -
Bb/C F Bb/C F Bb/C F
29
thy, wor - thy of our praise; We lift up our voice, we
Bbmaj7 Am7 Gm7 Am7 Bbmaj7 C F Bb/C
sing and re-joice; Lord, You're wor - thy of all of our praise.
F Bb13 A13 Ab13 G13 Bb/C F

34
VERSE
Praise Team
Hear, O Is - rael, the Lord God is One, the
C7(♭9)
Dm9
C7(♭9)
Am7
B♭maj7
C
King of kings and You reign up a - bove; Your pow - er and glo - ry shall
38
Dm9
Am7
B♭
C
Dm9
All
not be shared; All Heav - en and earth know that
Am7
B♭maj7
Gm7
F2/A
none can com - pare.
42
B♭maj7
C 7sus

1.
2.
C 7sus
D♭7sus
D♭
45
CHORUS 1
We lift You up,
we lift You up;
You're wor - thy, wor - thy
G♭5
C♭maj7
B♭m7
49
of our praise;
We lift You up,
we lift You up;
A♭m7 B♭m7 C♭maj7 A♭m7/D♭
G♭
C♭/D♭
G♭
Lord, You're wor - thy of all of our praise.
C♭13
B♭13
B♭♭13
A♭13
C♭/D♭
G♭

Medley options: Ain't Gonna Let No Rock; One True Living God.

....All things are possible to him who believes. Mark 9:23 (NKJV)

All Things Are Possible

Words and Music by
DARLENE ZSCHECH

like Je - sus, no pow'r can stand a - gainst You.
G Am7 G F G
17
My feet are plant - ed on this rock and I will not
C Am7 C
21
be shak - en; My hope, it comes from You a - lone,
Am7 G F G Am7 G
my Lord and my sal - va - tion.
F G Asus

CHORUS
Your praise is al - ways on my lips, Your Word is liv -
D
Bm7
D
29
ing in my heart; And I will praise
Bm7
G
You with a new song, my soul will bless
A
Bm7
A
G
33
You, Lord. You fill my life
Asus
D

with great - er joy, yes, I de - light
Bm7
D
37
my - self in You; And I will praise
Bm7
G
You with a new song, 1 my soul will bless
A
Bm7
A
G
41
You, Lord.
A
C
Am7

2, 3
my soul will bless
C
Am7
G
47
BRIDGE
You, Lord. When I am weak, You make me strong,
Asus
A
Bm7
D/A
G
when I'm poor I
D/F♯
G
51
know I'm rich; For in the pow - er of Your name
Bm7
A
Bm7
A
Asus
G

all things are pos - si - ble,
A7
55
all things are pos - si - ble;
All things are pos -
A7
D/A A7 D/A A7
last time to Coda
60
D.S.
si - ble,
all things are pos - si - ble.
A7
Coda
63
all things are pos - si - ble.
All things are pos -
A7
A7

Medley Options: I Can Do All Things; The Lord Reigns (STRADWICK).

1199

For He shall give his angels charge over you, to keep you in all your ways. Psalm 91:11 NKJ

Angels

Words and Music by
MARK CONDON

10
feel Your ho - ly pres - ence as Your glo - ry fills the air;
E♭maj7
B♭2/D
Cm7
15
I don't know where
E♭/F
B♭2
I would be if I had to walk a - lone, but
F2/A
F♯dim7
Gm
B♭/F
19
I have strength with You right there, know - ing I'm not on my own.
E♭maj7
B♭2/D
Cm7

I feel the an - gels o - ver
Cm7/F
Eb/F
25
CHORUS
me, they're walk - ing by my side; Through
Bb
Cm7
Bb2/D
ev - 'ry test of life, through ev - er - y vic - to - ry,
30
D7/F#
F#dim7
Gm
Bb/F
C/E
they are there with me; I feel the
F/Eb
Bb/D
Cm7(b5)

34
an - gels o - ver me, they're walk - ing by my
Cm7(♭5)/F
B♭
Cm7
38
side; Through ev - 'ry test of life, through
B♭2/D
D7/F♯
F♯dim7
Gm
42
ev - er - y vic - to - ry, they are there with me;
B♭/F
C/E
F/E♭
B♭/D
Cm7(♭5)
2nd time to Coda
45
I feel the an - gels o - ver me.
Cm7(♭5)/F
B♭

Cm7(add4)
B♭2/D
E♭/F
49
VERSE
Some-times it seemed to me that You are ver - y far a-way;
B♭2
F2/A
Gm7
53
But, al - ways just in time, You
B♭maj7/F
E♭maj7
B♭2/D
hear me when I pray;
57
Nev-er have You
E♭/A♭
F/A
B♭

ev - er failed to keep Your prom - is - es;
Am7
D(♭9)(♯11)
Gm9
B♭maj7/F
61
Through ev - 'ry test of life, my faith, it still stands.
3
E♭maj7
B♭2/D
Cm7
D.S. al Coda
I feel the an - gels o - ver
Cm7/F
66
Coda
B♭
Cm7(add4)
B♭2/D

His Eye Is On the Sparrow

Civilla D Martin and Charles H Gabriel

Medley options: Who's There, God's There.

Behold! The Lamb of God who takes away the sin of the world! John 1:29 (NKJ)

Behold The Lamb

Words and Music by
CRAIG SMITH

Medley options: Hallelujah; How Awesome Is Your Name.

1201

Come, let us bow down in worship, let us kneel before the Lord our Maker. Psalm 95:6 (NIV)

Bless This Time

Words and Music by
CRAIG CARTER

18
please, I won't let this time be in vain,
hour; Send Your a - noint - ing to bless,
E♭/G Cm7 F Gm7 F/A B♭
22
oh no; For I am de - ter - mined to love You,
For we are de - ter - mined to praise You,
C Dm E♭ B♭/D B♭ C
26
I'm com - mit - ted to bless Your name; So I
We're com - mit - ted to giv - ing our best; So we need
B♭ C E♭ B♭/D B♭/C C
30
CHORUS
Praise Team
ask You, Lord, Bless this time of praise,
You to bless
E♭ B♭/D Fsus/C F F Gm7 F/A B♭ E♭/B♭ B♭ F/A

34
38
Hon-or this moment of wor - ship; Touch each heart in this
Gm7 Dm7 F/B♭ C Dm7 C/E F F Gm7 F/A
42
3
place, Be glo - ri - fied in this ser -
B♭ E♭/B♭ B♭ F/A Gm7 Dm7 F6/C
46
vice; Bless this time, Bless this time of
C Dm7 C/E Gm7 F/G Fsus/G E♭ Dm7 Fsus/C
50
1.
praise.
2.We
F F7 B♭/F B♭m6/F

54
2.
praise.
F
F7
B♭
D♭
E♭
58
F
F7
B♭
Bless
this
62
time
of
D♭
E♭
F
F7
praise;
Bless
this
66
time,
B♭
D♭
E♭
F
3

Medley option: People of God.

Arise, O Lord! Deliver me, O my God. Psalm 3:7 (NIV)

Deliver Us

Words and Music by
CRAIG SMITH

wait-ing for his prey; Son of Da - vid, drive the e - vil one a - way.
bon-dag - es of sin; Je - sus Christ, we pray, de - liv - er us from him.
Em D/F♯ Am Dm G A
Band enters in tempo
10
De - liv - er us, a - rise,
De - li - ver us,
F F G Am
a - rise O God; De - liv - er us from e - vil,
Oh; De - li - ver us from e - vil,
F G Am F G Am G

14
de - liv - er us; De - liv - er us, a - rise,
Oh; De - li - ver us,
F G D/F♯ F G Am
a - rise O God; De - liv - er us from e - vil,
Oh; De - li - ver us from e - vil,
F G Am F G Am G
18
de - liv - er us; A - rise, de - liv - er us.
Oh; de - liv - er us.
F G D/F♯ F G

Medley options: Awesome God; We Have Overcome (KERR/MERKEL)

And ye shall seek me, and find me, when ye shall search for me with all your heart. Jeremiah 29:13 (KJV)

Draw Me Closer

Words and Music by
CRAIG SMITH

search-ing for Your cham - bers, to wor - ship You;
All
for the bread of Heav - en, Your breath of life;
B
E
A2
B
13
One ho - ly pas - sion for com - mun - ion, Lord.
W.L.
All
I seek Your ho - ly hab - i - ta - tion, Lord.
A2
B
E
17
CHORUS
Worship Leader & Congregation
Draw me clos - er to Your heart,
P.T.
Oo, to Your
E
C♯m7

21
draw me close to You;
Draw me clos - er
2nd time only
Both times
heart;
Draw me clos - er, Lord,
A2
Bsus
E
to Your heart,
draw me close to You.
1.
to Your heart.
C♯m7
A2
Bsus
2.
26
CHORUS - W.L. & Cong.
Draw me clos - er to Your heart,
Praise Team
Oo,
to Your
Bsus
E
C♯m7

draw me close to You;
30 Draw me clos - er
heart;
Draw me clos - er, Lord,
A2
Bsus
E
to Your heart,
draw me close to You.
to Your heart.
C♯m7
A2
Bsus
36 BRIDGE All
My Sav - ior,
E5
D5
I love You,
I wor - ship You;
E5
D5
E5

40
Worship Leader
Re-deem - er, how I long to be with You.
Praise Team
Re-deem - er, how I long to be with You.
Oo;
D5
E5
A2
44
Oh,
Oo.
B
A2/C♯
D2
46
CHORUS - W.L. & Cong.
Draw me clos - er to Your heart, draw me close to You;
Praise Team
Oo, to Your heart;
E
C♯m7
A2

Medley options: Adonai; More Of You (MERKEL).

Praise be to the LORD, the God of Israel, from everlasting to everlasting. 1 Chronicles 16:36 NIV

Everlasting

Words and Music by
PAUL SMITH

CHORUS - All
1st time - Melody and Tenor only
2nd & 3rd time - 3 part
9
Who for-ev - er-more shall reign.
Washing all my sins a - way.
Ev-er-last - ing is the
Gm7
Csus
C F2/A B♭2
Csus C
Lord, We will wor-ship and a - dore Lord Je-ho - vah still the
Dm
F2/A
B♭
Csus C
13
same;
Ev - er-last - ing, strong and
Dm
B♭2
Csus C
true, Lord, we put our trust in You, and with joy - ful hearts pro -
Dm
F2/A
B♭
Csus C

last time to Coda
1.
18
claim,
Ev - er - last - ing is Your name.
Dsus
D
Gm7
B♭/C
F
B♭
Dm
B♭2
2.
23
Ev - er - last - ing is Your name.
Gm7
B♭/C
B♭2
C
Dm7
C
27
E♭2

D.S. al Coda
B♭2/D
Gm7
Csus
C
F2/A
Coda
32
CHORUS - All
Ev - er-last - ing is Your
Ev - er-last - ing is the
Gm7
B♭/C
B♭2
Csus
C
Worship Leader ad libs
Lord, We will wor-ship and a - dore Lord Je-ho - vah still the
Dm
F2/A
B♭
Csus
C
36
All
same;
Ev - er-last - ing, strong and
Dm
B♭2
Csus
C

Medley options: Bow Down; Such Joy.

1205

Praise the Lord, all you servants of the LORD... Psa. 134:1 NIV

Everybody Praise the Lord

Words and Music by
LINCOLN BREWSTER

9
And I thank the Lord for what
A
He's gon-na do for us from the heav-ens a - bove;
13
And I thank the Lord for the smile
D
that He's put on my face; I thank the Lord for His grace;

17
And I thank the Lord for the joy
A
that He has giv - en to me, 'Cause now I know that I am
A
21
CHORUS
All
real - ly set free;
Ev - 'ry - bod - y, ev - 'ry - bod - y,
A
C2
Praise Team - Omit 1st time
ev - 'ry - bod - y praise the Lord;
Ooh,
D/F♯
G2
A
B/A

25
ooh;
Ev - 'ry - bod - y, ev - 'ry - bod - y,
Am7
D/A
A
C2
last time to Coda
1.
ev - 'ry-bod - y praise the Lord.
D/F#
G2
A
B/A
Am7
D/A
2.
Am7
D/A
D.S.
3.
Am7
D/A
A
A
33

35
N.C.
37
1.
2.
D.S. al Coda
Coda
41
CHORUS
1st time - Drums only
Ev - 'ry - bod - y, ev - 'ry - bod - y,
Am7
D/A
A
C2
ev - 'ry - bod - y praise the Lord;
Ooh,
D/F♯
G2
A
B/A

Medley options: Stand Up And Give Him The Praise.

Bless the LORD, O my soul; and all that is within me, bless his holy name. Psa. 103:1 NIV

Everything Within Me

Words and Music by
LYNN DESHAZO

13
ship You;
ship You;
These are feet of clay,
These are tears of joy,
A
But they will dance for You;
flow - ing down for You;
I wor -
I wor -
17
ship You,
ship You,
I wor - ship You;
I wor - ship You;
E
A
21
Here is my offer - ing of praise,
It's
D

25
Yours, Je - sus, my King;
Here is my heart,
D
A
D
How it is burst - ing to sing;
All
Let
B
E
29
CHORUS
Praise Team
All
ev - 'ry-thing with - in me,
(Ev - 'ry-thing with - in me)
Praise You for - ev - er;
A
E/A A
Praise Team
33
All
(Praise You for - ev - er)
ev - 'ry-thing with - in me,
re - joic - es in
F♯m
E D2

37
You.
Let ev - 'ry-thing with - in me
E
A
Praise Team
All
Praise Team
(Ev - 'ry-thing with - in me)
Praise You for - ev - er;
(Praise You for - ev - er)
F♯m
41
All
1.
Eve - ry - thing with - in me,
wor - ships You.
D
E
A2
45
D2

2.
Worship Leader ad libs
49
F♯m
D
A
E
F♯m
D
55
CHORUS
Let
ev-'ry-thing with-in me,
Esus
E
F♯sus
F♯
B
3
Praise Team
All
58
Praise Team
(Ev-'ry-thing with-in me)
Praise You for-ev-er;
(Praise You for-ev-er)
B
F♯/B
B

All
Ev - 'ry-thing with - in me, re - joic - es in You;
G♯m
F♯
E2
F♯
63
Let ev - 'ry-thing with - in me
Praise Team
(Ev - 'ry-thing with - in me)
B
All
Praise You for - ev - er;
Praise Team
(Praise You for - ev - er)
67
All
Ev - 'ry-thing with - in me,
G♯m
E
1.
2.
Let
wor - ships You.
F♯
B

72
All
Ev - 'ry-thing with - in me, wor - ships You.
B2/D♯ E2
F♯sus F♯
76
Ev - 'ry-thing with - in me,
G♯m E2 B2/D♯ C♯m
wor - ships You.
F♯sus B
80
Worship Leader
Hands of love, I lift them up to You,
B

Medley options: For The Lord Is Good: Sing Out.

1207

Know therefore that the LORD your God is God; he is the faithful God, keeping his covenant of love to a thousand generations... Deuteronomy 7:9 NIV

Faithful God

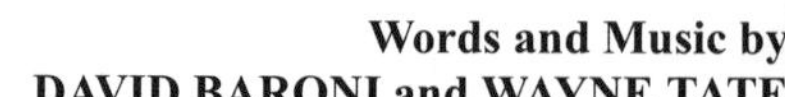

Words and Music by
DAVID BARONI and WAYNE TATE

♩= 60

B♭ C Dm B♭ C/E F F/A

Worship Leader

As the

B♭ C Dm7 B♭2

5 *VERSE*
2nd time - Worship Leader and Ladies

sun is re - born, and a beau - ti - ful morn - ing re - minds

F B♭6/F

2nd time - Men add harmony

me of Your faith - ful - ness to me; Through the

C F B♭2/D

9
long, lone - ly night,
when the dark - ness hid the light,
You
F
B♭6/F
gave me grace to trust
and now I see;
E-ven when it's
C
F
13
2nd time - 3 part
hard to be-lieve,
e-ven when our
hope seems all gone,
there has
B♭maj7
F/A
nev - er been a night
with-out a dawn.
All
Faith - ful God,
E♭
B♭/D
C 7sus

17
CHORUS
un - fail - ing love,
for -
F
C/E
Dm
ev - er You are worth - y of our praise;
Faith - ful God,
Gm7
C7sus
C
21
un - fail - ing love,
We can
F
C/E
Dm
al - ways trust the wis - dom of Your ways,
Faith - ful God,
Gm7
C7sus

1.
Worship Leader
Faith - ful, Faith - ful God.
Praise Team Men
Faith - ful God.
B♭ C Dm B♭ C/E F F/A
27
Worship Leader and Ladies
As the
Praise Team
Faith - ful God.
B♭ C Dm7 B♭2
2.
Worship Leader
The
Faith - ful God.
B♭2

31
BRIDGE
All
hea - vens, they are tell - ing of the glo - ry of our King, So we
Heav - ens, tell - ing, glo - ry of our King;
F/A
B♭
C
Dm7
33
join with all cre - a - tion now and sing; Faith - ful God,
E♭
B♭/D
Csus
C
35
CHORUS
un - fail - ing love, for-
G
D/F♯
Em

ev - er You are worth - y of our praise; Faith - ful God,
Am7
D 7sus
39
un - fail - ing love,
We can
G
D/F♯
Em
Em/D
al - ways trust the wis - dom of Your ways,
1.
Faith - ful God,
Am7
D 7sus
D/F♯

2.
44
Worship Leader ad libs
ways, Faith - ful God;
Praise Team Men
Faith - ful God.
D 7sus
D
C
D
Em
Praise Team Women
Faith - ful God;
Faith - ful God.
C
D/F♯
G
G/B
C
D
Em
48
Faith - ful God,
Faith - ful God.
C
D/F♯
G
G/B
C
D
Em

Faith - ful God;

Faith - ful God.

C D/F♯ G G/B C D Em

Worship Leader

You're Faith - ful, Faith - ful God.

C Cmaj7/E D/F♯ G

Medley options: We Need Your Presence; Be Magnified.

Our Father which art in heaven, Hallowed be thy name. Matthew 6:9 (KJV)

Father

Words and Music by
CRAIG SMITH

13
there is no one like You;
You call us the children of God;
A2 E D2
17
Add Ladies, bottom note
Fa - ther, E - ter - nal
W.L.
Add Praise Team, lower notes
Fa - ther, Pro - tec - tor, Pro -
Bsus A2 E
Add Ladies, bottom note
21
Fa - ther, We bow
vid - er, our lives
A2 E A2 E

our hearts be - fore You;
are des - tined in You;
You
D2
Bsus
25
All
Fa - ther of lights, our hope, our fu - ture,
care - ful - ly nur - ture the lives of Your chil - dren,
A
B
We rest se - cure - ly in You.
W.L.
Fa - ther, You
Safe in Your arms we a - bide.
Fa - ther, You
A
B

29
CHORUS
W.L.
are Lord of the heav - ens; You are Lord of the
Praise Team
are, You are;
E
A
C♯m7
earth; Fa - ther, You are God in the high - est; You
33
Fa - ther, You are, You
B
E
A
are God of all life;
1.
37
For - ev - er our Fa - ther You
are, You
C♯m7
A2

40
are.
are.
E5
43
2, 3.
CHORUS
life; Fa - ther, You are Lord of the
You are,
A2
E
heav - ens; You are Lord of the earth; Fa - ther, You
You are; Fa - ther, You
A
C♯m7
B

47
last time to Coda
are God in the high - est; You are God of all
are, You are,
E
A
C♯m7
life; For - ev - er our Fa - ther You are.
For - ev - er our Fa - ther You are.
A2
E5
54
BRIDGE
You're the Ho - ly, Right - eous
Ho - ly, Right - eous
G2
A2

58
One,
Faith - ful,
One,
Faith - ful,
E
G2
Fa - ther,
God.
Fa - ther,
God.
A2
B5
3
64
Fa - ther,
You are
You are,
3
E

God in the high - est;
Oo, You
You
A2
68
are
God of all life;
are,
C♯m7
B
Fa - ther, You are
72
God in the high -
You are,
E

76
est;
You are
You are,
A2
C♯m7
77
God of all life;
B
80
D.S. al Coda
Oh;
Fa - ther, You
A2

Medley options: Open The Eyes Of My Heart; Only God For Me.

1209

Have mercy on me, O God, according to your unfailing love. Psalm 51:1 (NIV)

Father Of Life

Words and Music by
CRAIG SMITH

13
seek, My spir - it is thirst - ing; Please re-move my trans-gres -
W.L. and Praise Team Ladies
My heart needs Your mend - ing; Please re-move my trans-gres -
A2
Bsus
D/F♯
sions, cleanse me from my sin.
W.L.
sions, For-give me, O God.
A2
D/F♯
B2
17
CHORUS
All
Fa - ther of Life, please have mer -
A2
Bsus

21
cy,
Take this heart and give
E2
A2
it pur - i - ty;
B2
E2
25
All
Fa - ther of Life, pour Your mer - cy o - ver me,
A2
B2
E2
29
and re - new a stead - fast spir - it with - in me.
A2
B2

last time to Coda
1.
2.
E2
34
BRIDGE
W.L.
Re-ceive my sac - ri-fice,
All
a bro-ken spir -
C2/G
D2
C2/E
38
D.S. al Coda
it, bro-ken heart.
D/F♯
Bsus
Coda
41
and re-new a stead - fast spir - it with-in me.
E2
A2/C♯
B

Medley options: I Give You My Heart; Let Your Spirit Come.

For the earth will be filled with the knowledge of the glory of the Lord. Habakkuk 2:14 (NKJ)

Fill The Earth

Words and Music by
CRAIG SMITH

prayer, pour out Your Spir - it ev - 'ry - where;
land, let right-eous-ness pre - vail a - gain;
grace, to be raised up in ev - 'ry place;
Fm7
Eb/G
Ab2
Bb
Cm
13
Let Je - sus bold - ly be pro - claimed,
Re - deem the stand - ard of Your will,
All
For ev - 'ry na - tion, ev - 'ry tongue,
1.
17
and ev - 'ry heart con - fess His Name.
may Your de - sires be ful -
to bow be - fore the Cho - sen
Eb

Fm7
E♭/G
A♭2
B♭
Cm
2, 3.
22
All
(Melody top note)
filled.
(2.) We
ap - peal
be - fore
All
(Melody top note)
One.
(3.) With
one
voice,
one
ho -
E♭
Fm7
E♭/G
26
Your
throne,
let
Mes - si -
ly
aim,
free
the world,
A♭
B♭
Fm7

ah's Name be known.
in Je - sus' Name.
Eb/G
Ab
Bb
30
CHORUS
All
Fill the earth with Your glo - ry, Lord,
C2
Ab
Fm7
34
Fill the world
Bb
B5
C2
Fm7

1.
38
with the rev - e - la - tion of Your Son.
A♭2
B♭2
Gm7
C2
B♭
Gm
42
All ad lib
C2
B♭
Gm
C2
B♭
Gm
C2
Fm7
E♭/G
A♭2
B♭
Fm7
E♭/G
A♭2
B♭
Cm
2.
48
CHORUS
2nd time W.L. ad libs
with Your rev - e - la - tion.
Fill the earth
A♭2
B♭2
Gm7
C2

49
with Your glo - ry, Lord,
A♭
Fm7
B♭
B5
52
1.
Fill the world
with the rev - e - la -
C2
Fm7
A♭2
B♭2
57
tion of Your Son.
Gm7
C2
B♭
Gm
C2
B♭
Gm
2.
with Your rev - e - la -
C2
B♭
Gm
C2
B♭
Gm
A♭2
B♭2

62
CHORUS
W.L. ad libs
tion.
Fill the earth
Gm7
C2
A♭
with Your glo - ry, Lord,
66
Fill the world
Fm7
B♭
B5
C2
with Your rev - e - la - tion,
Fm7
A♭2
B♭2
70
with Your rev - e - la - tion,
A♭2
B♭2

Medley options: We Declare That The Kingdom Of God Is Here.

Love the LORD your God with all your heart and with all your soul and with all your strength. Deuteronomy 6:5 NIV

Giving My Best

Words and Music by
MARK CONDON

none to be found; To think that the price You
so pa - tient - ly, my heart is filled with such
F/A
G
C
paid for me was - n't in vain, all that
love for You, and I know the best thing for
G/B
Gm/B♭
a - go - ny; But,
me to do; I
F/A
F/G
G

15
3
I'm here to say I've had my ups and my downs, but I'm
come to You, Lord, to an - swer Your call; O, I'm
Fmaj7
G/F
here now to stay 'cause of the love that I found. Now, I'm
not hold - ing back, but I'm giv - ing my all. Now, I'm
C/E
Dm
Dm7/G
G
20
CHORUS
All
giv - ing my best to You, Lord, all that I have
C
Em7
Am7
D9

Ladies
24
All
I won't with-hold;
Giv-ing my best to You, Lord,
Dm7
F/G
C
Em7
last time to Coda
1.
P.T.
all of my heart
and all of my soul.
Am7
D9
Dm7/G
C
Dm/C
W.L.
2.
2. When I
and all of my soul.
Ddim7/C
C
Dm7/G
C
32
BRIDGE
P.T.
W.L. ad libs
You are the One that tru-ly did it for me;
You gave Your best at
E♭maj7/F
B♭maj9
G+7(♯9)
Cm9
E♭maj7/F

36
Cal - va - ry.
You are the One that made that sac - ri - fice;
B♭maj9
Emaj7/F
E♭maj7/F
B♭maj9
3
So, now I'm giv - ing my best,
I'm giv - ing my
Cm7
B♭2/D
E♭
40
D.S. al Coda
W.L.
Now I'm
life; I'll give my life.
Csus/D
F/G
⊕ Coda
All
43
W.L.
and all of my soul.
I'm giv - ing my
Dm7/G
C
Dm/C
Ddim7/C
C

45
BRIDGE 2
P.T.
W.L. ad libs
best; I'm giv-ing my best,
I'm here to give You all;
F/C
Ev - 'ry-thing in me, Lord,
I won't with-hold;
W.L.
I'm giv-ing my
Dm7(♭5)/C
C
G/C
C
F/G
49
P.T.
W.L. ad libs
best; I'm giv-ing my best,
I'm here to give You all;
C
F/C
Ev - 'ry-thing in me, Lord,
I won't with-hold;
W.L.
I'm giv-ing my
Dm7(♭5)/C
C
G/C
C
F/G

53
P.T.
best; I'm giv - ing my best, I'm here to give You all;
C
F/C
W.L.
Ev - 'ry-thing in me, Lord, I won't with - hold; I'm giv - ing my
Dm7(♭5)/C
C G/C C
F/G
57
P.T.
best; I'm giv - ing my best, I'm here to give You all;
C
F/C
Ev - 'ry-thing in me, Lord, I won't with - hold.
Dm7(♭5)/C
C G/C C
G♭/A♭

61
CHORUS
P.T.
W.L. ad libs
I'm giv-ing my best to You, Lord, all that I have
D♭
Fm7
B♭m7
E♭9
Ladies
All
I won't with-hold; Now I'm
E♭m7
G♭/A♭
Gmaj7/A
A9
G/A
66
CHORUS
W.L. ad libs
giv-ing my best to You, Lord, all that I have
D
F♯m7
Bm7
E9
Ladies
70
All
W.L. ad libs
I won't with-hold; Giv-ing my best to You, Lord,
Em7
G/A
D
F♯m7

Medley options: Hallowed Be Your Name (KENOLY/SMITH).

....Where sin increased, grace increased all the more. Romans 5:20 (NIV)

Grace, Greater Than Our Sin

Words and Music by
JULIA H. JOHNSTON
and DANIEL B. TOWNER

13
grace; Grace that is great - er than
F(add2) Gm/B♭ D7/A Gm7 F/A Gm/B♭
18
all our sin. Grace,
F/C C F C/D G(add2)
grace, God's grace;
G(add2)/B C(add2) G(add2)
22
Grace that will par - don and cleanse with -
D C(add2) G/B Am7

Medley Options: Above All; But for Your Grace.

The Lord reigns, he is robed in majesty... Psalm 93:1 (NIV)

Hallelujah

Words and Music by
CRAIG SMITH

9
W.L.
Your eyes blaze like fire (re), crowns up - on Your head,
King of the A - ges, Bright and Morn - ing Star,
G
D/F♯
1st time W.L. only, lower note
2nd time add P.T. Men, upper note
All (Melody top note)
You are the Word of God, the Be - gin - ning and the End. Hal - le -
Won - der - ful Coun - se - lor, all of life is in Your charge.
Asus
A
13
CHORUS
lu - jah, our Lord Al - might - y reigns; Je - sus
Christ our Sav - ior reigns; Hal - le -

Medley options: Behold The Lamb (SMITH); I Come To You.

1214

Worthy is the Lamb, who was slain, to receive power and wealth and wisdom
and strength and honor and glory and praise! Revelation 5:12 (NIV)

He Alone Is Worthy

Words and Music by
ART BAIN

Li-on of the tribe of Ju - dah, Je-sus Christ, the Son.
B♭ C/B♭ Am7 Dm7 F/G G Gm7 C7sus C
12
CHORUS 1st time - Unison
2nd time - Parts
He a - lone is worth - y to wor - ship and a -
F F/A B♭ F/C Gm/C F C7 F Am7
dore, The Lamb of God, vic - tor - i - ous, our
B♭ F7 B♭ E♭/B♭ B♭ F
20
ri - sen Lord; He pur - chased our re -
F/A Csus C7 F F/A B♭ F/C C7

24
demp-tion, our right-eous-ness is He; Ex - alt the name of
F C7 F Am7 B♭ F7 B♭ E♭/B♭ B♭
Je - sus, He is worth - y.
F F/A B♭ F/C C7sus C F
1.
28
2.
y.
F F/E♭ D D7/C
Gm/B♭ Asus A Dsus D D/F♯
32
Instrumental Solo
G G/B C G/D Am/D

G D7 G Bm7 C G7
36 C F/C C G G/B
All 40
He pur - chased our re - demp - tion, our
Dsus D7 G G/B C G/D D7 G D7
44
right - eous - ness is He; Ex - alt the name of
G Bm7 C G7 C F/C C

Je - sus, He is worth - y.
G G/B C G/D D7sus D G D♭/E♭
48
CHORUS
He a - lone is worth - y to wor - ship and a -
A♭ A♭/C D♭ A♭/E♭ B♭m/E♭ A♭ E♭7 A♭ Cm7
52
dore, The Lamb of God, vic - tor - i - ous, our
D♭ A♭7 D♭ G♭/D♭ D♭ A♭
56
ri - sen Lord; He pur - chased our re -
A♭/C E♭sus E♭7 A♭ A♭/C D♭ A♭/E♭ E♭7

demp - tion, our right - eous - ness is He; Ex -
A♭ E♭7 A♭ Cm7 D♭ A♭7
60
alt the name of Je - sus, He is worth -
D♭ G♭/D♭ D♭ A♭ A♭/C D♭ A♭/E♭ E♭7sus E♭
64
y; Ex - alt the Name of Je - sus, He is
A♭ A♭7 D♭ G♭/D♭ D♭ A♭ A♭/C D♭
worth - y; He is worth -
A♭/E♭ E♭7sus E♭ A♭ D♭/F A♭/C B♭m/D♭ A♭/E♭ E♭7sus E♭

Medley options: O The Blood of Jesus; By Your Blood (FUNK).

The LORD is good to those whose hope is in Him... Lamentations 3:25 NIV

He's Been Good

Words and Music by
DAVID BARONI

13
all, He's al - ways there for me, God's been good to me.
F Gm7 F/A B♭ F/C C11
1 2
VERSE
Worship Leader
16
I have Through the storm, through the
B♭/F F C11 B♭/F F Am7 Dm7
night, come what may, ev - 'ry - thing will
Gm7 C11 Am7 Dm7
All
20
be all right; I have known the Fa - ther's care for me,
Gm7 C11 F Gm7 F/A B♭

D.S. al Coda
3
He's been good to me. I have
F/C C11 B♭/F F C11 B♭/F F D11
INSTRUMENTAL
25
G Am7 G/B C G Em7
Am7 D11
29
G Am7 G/B C
32
VERSE
Worship Leader
Through the storm, through the
G/D D11 C/G G Bm7 Em7

night, come what may, ev - 'ry - thing will
Am7 D11 Bm7 Em7
36
All
be all right; I have known the Fa - ther's care
Am7 D11 G Am7 G/B C
for me, He's been good to me.
G/D D11 C/G G
41 BRIDGE
Good, so good, God's been good to me,
F/G C/G Cm6/G

Medley Options: How Great Is Your Goodness; Jesus, Lover Of My Soul

1216

Holy, holy, holy is the Lord God Almighty, who was, and is, and is to come. Revelation 4:8 (NIV)

Holy Is The Lord

9
the Li-on of the Tribe of Ju - dah, the
You're the Cap - tain and Com - mand - er,
A2
root of Da - vid is the King of kings; To
Mas - ter and Mes - si - ah, Son of God;
E
B2
13
W.L. & Men
All
Him Who sits up - on the throne and un - to the Lamb,
W.L. & Men
All
Let the re - deemed bow down and wor - ship the Lamb,
A2
E
B2

W.L. & Men
17
be bless - ing, do - min - ion and
W.L. & Men
with bless - ing, do - mi - nion and
A2
All
glo - ry and hon - or for - ev - er.
W.L.
3
And we cry
glo - ry and hon - or for - ev - er.
E
B2
21
CHORUS
All
ho - ly, ho - ly,
A2
E
B2

25
ho - ly is the Lord;
A2
E
B2
29
Who was,
A2
E
33
Who is, and Who
B2
A2
last time to Coda
1.
is to come.
E
B2

2.
38
BRIDGE
W.L.
Let us re - joice, our God Al - might - y reigns;
A2
Praise Team
Let us re - joice,
Let us re - joice, our God Al - might - y reigns;
B2
A2
45
our God Al - might - y reigns;
Let us re - joice, our God Al - might - y,
B2
B2

46
Let us re - joice,
Ev - 'ry knee will soon bow down, ev - 'ry tongue con - fess that Je - sus
A2
for our God reigns;
49
Christ is Lord;
Ev - 'ry,
B2
50
Let us re - joice.
Ev - 'ry knee will soon bow down, ev - 'ry tongue con - fess that Je - sus
A2

54
Christ is Lord;
B2
A2
E
B2
1.
2.
W.L.
D.S. al Coda
3
O,
and we cry
B2
Coda
61
and Who is to
A2
E

Medley options: Prepare The Way; Celebrate The Lord of Love.

1217

That at the name of Jesus every knee should bow....and every tongue confess that Jesus Christ is Lord... Philippians 2:10, 11 NIV

Holy Is Thy Name

Words and Music by
MARK CONDON

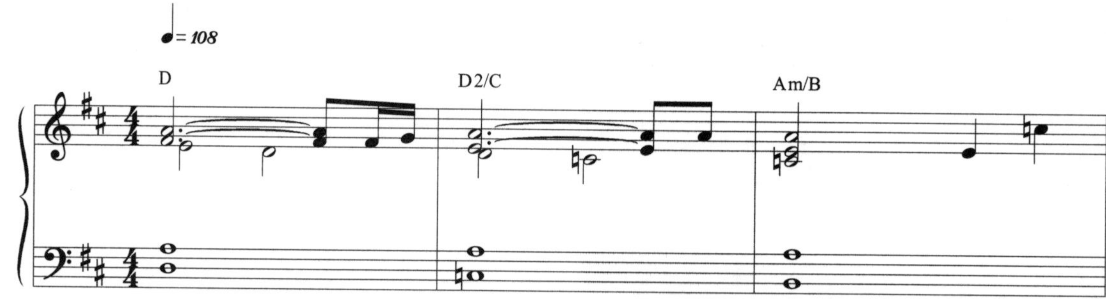

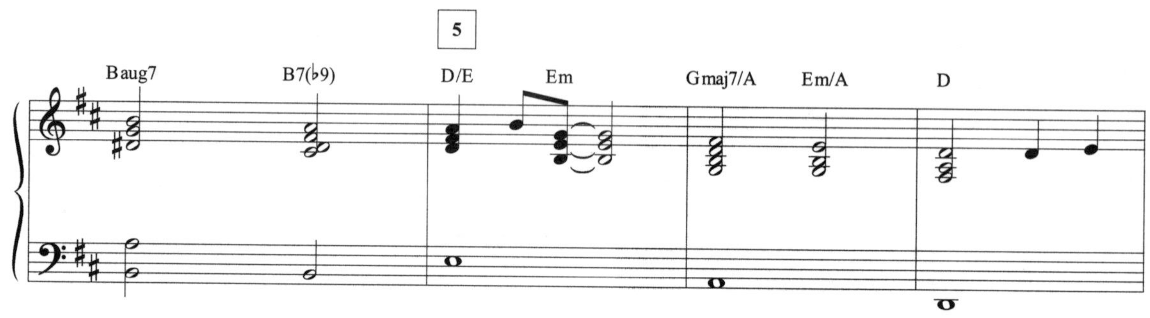

13
How mar - vel - ous and glo - ri - ous
D
Am/C
B7
D/E
Em7
1.
Praise Team
is Thy Ho - ly Name.
Ho - ly is Thy Name,
D/A
Em7/A
D
B7(♭9)
2.
There's heal - ing in that Name,
D
B7(♭9)
19
CHORUS
21
heal - ing in that Name; How
pow - er in that Name; How
Em7
A 7sus
D
Am/C

1.
mar - vel - ous and glo - ri - ous is Thy Ho - ly Name.
mar - vel - ous and glo - ri - ous
B7
D/E
Em7
D/A
Em7/A
D
27
VERSE
W.L.
There's no oth - er Name than my
Bm
B♭aug
Gm/B♭
D/A
31
Je - sus; That pre - cious, Ho - ly Name,
G♯m7(♭5)
Gm6
D/F♯

3
35
it can set you free.
There's pow - er in that Name,
P.T.
There's
Em7
Asus
A
2.
is Thy Ho - ly Name.
pow - er in that Name,
B7(♭9)
D/A
Em7/A
D
39
CHORUS
Je - sus is that Name,
How I love that Name,
Je - sus is that Name;
how I love that Name;
B7(♭9)
Em7
A 7sus

43
How mar - vel - ous and glo - ri - ous
How mar - vel - ous and glo - ri - ous
D
Am/C
B7
D/E
Em7
1.
2.
is Thy Ho - ly Name.
is Thy Ho - ly Name.
D/A
Em7/A
D
D
49
Bdim7
Cm7
F7
B♭
Dm7(♭5)/A♭
G7

Cm
B♭/F
F7
B♭
56
CHORUS
1st time, W.L.
2nd time, P.T.
W.L. ad libs
P.T.
Je - sus is that Name,
Je - sus is that Name;
How I love that Name,
how I love that Name;
C7(♭9)
Fm7
B♭7sus
60
How mar - vel - ous and glo - ri - ous
How mar - vel - ous and glo - ri - ous
E♭
B♭m/D♭
C7
E♭/F
Fm7
1.
is Thy Ho - ly Name.
is Thy Ho - ly Name.
E♭/B♭
Fm7/B♭
E♭

Medley options: Your Name Is Jesus.

...No eye has seen, no ear has heard, no mind has conceived what God has prepared for those who love Him. I Corinthians 2:9 (NIV)

Holy Spirit Rain Down

Words and Music by
RUSSELL FRAGAR

13
Com - fort - er and Friend, How we need Your touch a - gain;
Am7
G2/B
C
17
Ho - ly Spir - it rain down,
Dsus
G
F/G
rain down; Let Your pow - er fall, Let Your
21
F/C
C
G/D
voice be heard, Come and change our hearts as we stand on Your Word; Ho - ly
23
D♯dim7
Em
Am7(♭5)/E♭

5
a tempo
Spir - it, rain down.
G/D
C/D
D2/F♯
C/G
D/G
3
All
29
CHORUS
Ho - ly Spir - it rain down,
G
C/D
G
F/G
33
rain down; O Com - fort - er and Friend,
F/C
C
G/B
Am7
How we need Your touch a - gain; Ho - ly Spir - it
G2/B
C
Dsus

37
rain
down,
rain
G
F/G
F/C
41
down;
Let Your
pow - er fall,
Let Your
voice be heard,
Come and
C
G/D
D♯dim7
45
change our hearts
as we
stand on Your Word;
Ho - ly
Spir -
Em
Am7(♭5)/E♭
G/D
1, 2.
it,
rain
down.
C/D
C/G
G
D/G

49
VERSE
Worship Leader
No eye has seen, No ear has heard, No mind can know what
C
B7
B7/D♯
Em7
53
God has in store, so o-pen up Hea - ven, o-pen it wide,
Dm7
F/G
C
B7
B7/D♯
o - ver Your Church and o - ver our lives.
Em7
D 7sus
57
All
3.
Ho - ly Spir - it down.
D 7sus
C2

Worship Leader
60
Let Your pow - er fall, Let Your voice be heard, Come and
D/C
G/D
D♯dim7
62
change our hearts as we stand on Your Word; Ho - ly
Em7
Am7(♭5)/E♭
Am7(♭5)/E♭
8va
65
Sung 1st time only
Spir - it, rain down.
G/D
D7sus
C2
68
D/C
C
D/C

Medley options: I Want To Be Where You Are; We Need Your Presence.

1219

I love you, O LORD, my strength. Psalm 18:1 NIV

I'm Loving You More Each Day

Words and Music by
MARK CONDON

9
di - rect - ed me;
There's not a val - ley
my yes - ter-days;
For I have a hope that
Gm7
C
that I've gone through
that I just grow strong - er in
this too shall pass,
and when I'm on top,
I'll know I've
A7(♭9)
D m2
Dm/C
13
my walk with You.
So, with all of my heart,
Lord,
I say,
made it at last;
And, Lord,
You will hear me
Bm7(♭5)
Gm7

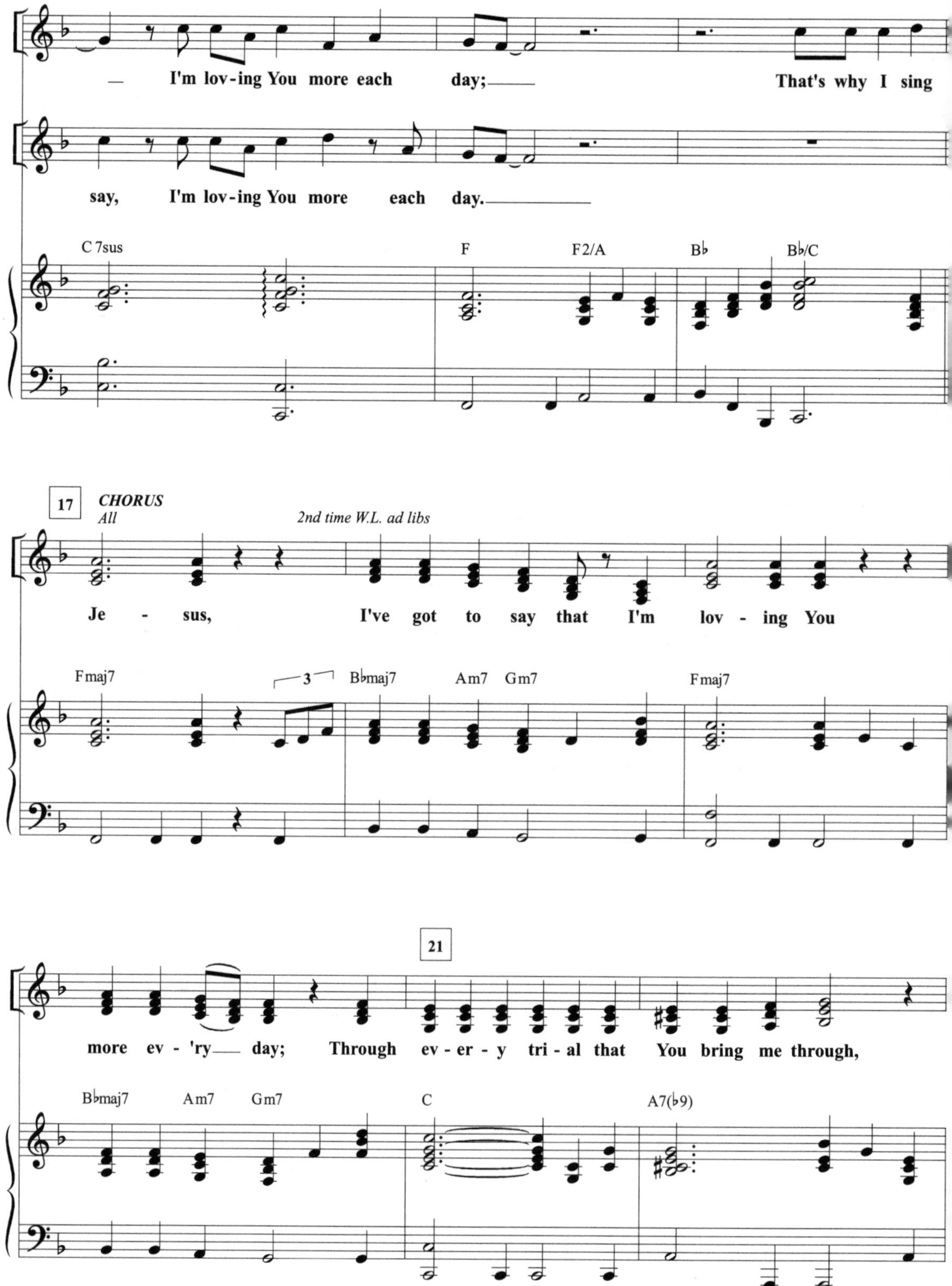

I'm lov-ing You more each day; That's why I sing
say, I'm lov-ing You more each day.
C 7sus
F
F2/A
B♭
B♭/C
17
CHORUS
All
2nd time W.L. ad libs
Je - sus, I've got to say that I'm lov - ing You
Fmaj7
3
B♭maj7
Am7
Gm7
Fmaj7
21
more ev - 'ry day; Through ev - er - y tri - al that You bring me through,
B♭maj7
Am7
Gm7
C
A7(♭9)

my love grows strong - er and strong - er for You; So, with
Dm Dm/C Bm7(♭5)

25
all of my heart, Lord, I say, All I'm lov - ing You more each
Gm7 F/A B♭ C7sus

1.
day. W.L. 2. When the
F F2/A B♭maj7 B♭/C

2.
day.
F F2/A B♭2 B♭/C

31
BRIDGE
P.T.
W.L. ad libs
Thank You, thank You;
F
Faug
Thank You, thank You, for ev-'ry val-ley that has come my
W.L.
35
Dm/F
D7(♯9)
Gm7
All
way, I'm lov-ing You more each day.
1.
B♭/C
F
F2/A
B♭2
B♭/C
2.
40
CHORUS
P.T.
W.L. ad libs
Je - sus, I've got to say that I'm
B♭2
C♭/D♭
G♭maj7
C♭maj7
B♭m7
A♭m7

44
lov - ing You more ev - 'ry day; Through ev - er - y tri - al that
G♭maj7
C♭maj7
B♭m7
A♭m7
D♭
W.L.
3
You bring me through, my love grows strong-er and strong-er for You; So, with
B♭7(♭9)
E♭m
E♭m/D♭
Cm7(♭5)
48
P.T.
all of my heart, Lord, I say, I'm lov-ing You more each
A♭m7
G♭/B♭
C♭
D♭7sus
W.L. ad libs
day. I'm lov - ing You more each
G♭
G♭2/B♭
C♭maj7
C♭/D♭

Medley options: My Heart Will Trust; Jesus, Name Above All Names.

...This same Jesus, who has been taken from you into heaven, will come back in the same way you have seen him go into heaven. Acts 1:11 (NIV)

I'm Talking 'Bout Jesus

Words and Music by
CRAIG YOUNG and
ANTHONY HERRGESELL

11
Just turn your eyes to the sky up a - bove;
Just like the child - ren of the Prom - ised Land, If
B
G♯m7
E
B
He chang - es not, He chang - es not. I'm talk - ing 'bout
He leads us out, I know that He leads us in.
E
B
E
B
15
CHORUS
Je - sus, Glo - ry, Right-eous, Ho - ly,
Praise Team
Je - sus, Glo - ry, Right - eous, Ho - ly,
B
G♯m7
B
G♯m7

Lamb of God, Some-day He's com - ing a - gain; I'm sing-ing 'bout
Lamb of God, He's com - ing a - gain;
B G♯m7 E B/D♯ C♯m7 B
19
Je - sus, Sav - ior, Heal - er, Mak - er,
Je - sus, Sav - ior, Heal - er, Mak-er,
B G♯m7 B G♯m7
1.
War-ri-or, Praise God, He's com - ing a - gain.
War-ri-or, He's com-ing a - gain.
B G♯m7 E B/D♯ C♯m7 B

24
BRIDGE
2.
com - ing a - gain.
Praise Team
Let the king-dom come;
E B/D♯ C♯m7 B
B Gdim7 G♯m7
All
Hal-le-lu-jah;
Praise Team
Let the king-dom come;
All
Hal-le-lu-jah;
N.C.
B Gdim7 G♯m7
N.C.
28
Worship Leader
When we have Heav-en here on earth, then we'll be done.
C♯m7
Em(+7) Emin6

31
Je - sus, yeah.
Praise Team
Ooo, Oh, oh;
Dmaj7
C♯m7
Cmaj7
B
35
Yeah.
Ooo, Oh, oh; Yeah.
E7
Dmaj7
C♯m7 Cmaj7
B
Talk - ing 'bout
Ooo, Oh, oh;
E7
Dmaj7
C♯m7
F♯7sus

39
CHORUS
Je - sus, Je - sus, say Je - sus, Je - sus,
Je - sus, Je - sus, Je - sus, Je - sus,
B G♯m7 B G♯m7
41
D.S.
Lamb of God, Some-day He's com-ing a-gain; and I'm sing-ing 'bout
Lamb of God, He's com-ing a-gain;
B G♯m7 E B
43
3.
com - ing a - gain; I said, His name is Je-sus, Sav-ior,
com - ing a - gain; Je-sus, Sav-ior,
E B/D♯ C♯m7 B B G♯m7

45
Heal - er,
Mak - er,
War-ri - or,
Praise God,
He's
Heal - er,
Mak - er,
War-ri - or,
He's
B
G♯m7
B
G♯m7
com - ing
a - gain;
Yes, He's
My God
is,
com - ing
a - gain;
He's
com - ing
a - gain;
He's
E
B/D♯
C♯m7
B
E
B/D♯
C♯m7
B
Praise Team
50
com - ing
a - gain.
Ooo,
E
B/D♯
C♯m7
B
Dmaj7

Medley option: Righteousness, Peace, Joy.

For where two or three come together in my name, there am I with them. Matthew 18:20 (NIV)

I Believe the Promise

Words and Music by
RUSSELL FRAGAR

11
That the Ho - ly Spir - it will be poured out and His
Bm7
D/E
F♯m7 Gmaj7
15
pow - er will be seen;
Well the time is now, and the place
Second time Praise Team
Ooo,
G/A
D
is here, and His peo - ple have come in faith;
There's a might -
Ooo;
Might -
Gm/D
D
A/C♯ Bm7

19
y sound and a touch of fire (re) when we gath-er in one place.
y Touch of fire (re)
Em7
A 7sus
23
CHORUS
I be - lieve that the pre-sence of
Praise Team both times
I be - lieve pre-sence of
A
D
F♯7(♯5)
Bm7
D7/A
27
God is here;
There's not one thing that can't
God is here;
G
D
F♯m7

be changed
When the Spir-it of God is near;
Bm7
Em7
G
A 7sus
31
I be-lieve that the pre-sence of God is here;
I be-lieve pre-sence of God is here;
D
F♯7(♯5)
Bm7
D7/A
G
D
35
Where two or three are gath-ered, When
Ooo,
Em7
F♯m7
Bm7
F♯m7
Em7

39
peo - ple a - rise in faith,
I be - lieve God an -
Ooo,
F♯m7
Bm7
F♯m7
Em7
F♯m7
swers,
and His pres - ence is in this place.
1.
and His pres - ence is in this place.
Bm7
F♯m7
Em7
G/A
C/D
D♭/E♭
D/E
43
BRIDGE
2.
Noth - ing on earth or Heav - en
Can stop the pow'r
Noth - ing on earth or Heav - en
Can stop the pow'r
C/D
D/E
C/D

47
of God;
In - to our hands is giv - en
of God;
In - to our hands is giv - en
B♭/C B/C♯ C/D
D/E
the call to take it on;
51
No o - cean
the call to take it on;
No o - cean
C/D
D♭/E♭ D/E
can con-tain it,
No star can rise a - bove;
can con-tain it,
No star can rise a - bove;
E/F♯ D/E
C/D D♭/E♭ D/E

55
In - to our hearts is giv - en
The pow'r of His love.
In - to our hearts is giv - en
The pow'r of His love.
E/F♯ Bm7 A A2/C♯
59
CHORUS
I be-lieve that the pre-sence of
I be-lieve that the pre-sence of
B2/D♯ E G♯7(♯5) C♯m7 E7/B
63
God is here;
There's not one thing that can't
God is here;
A E G♯m7

– be — changed —
No, —
When the Spir - it of God — is — near; —
C♯m7
F♯m7
A
B 7sus
67
I be - lieve — that the pre - sence of God — is here; —
I be - lieve — pre - sence of God — is here; —
E
G♯7(♯5)
C♯m7
E7/B
A
E
71
All
Where two or three are gath - ered, —
When peo - ple a - rise — in — faith, —
Ooo, —
F♯m7
G♯m7
C♯m7
G♯m7
F♯m7
G♯m7

75
I be-lieve God an - swers and His
Ooo, and His
C♯m7 G♯m7 F♯m7 G♯m7 C♯m7 G♯m7 F♯m7
1.
pres-ence is in this place. I be - lieve that the pre-sence of
pres-ence is in this place. I be - lieve that the pre-sence of
A/B E G♯7(♯5) C♯m7 E7/B
80
2.
pres - ence is in this place. In this place;
pres - ence is in this place.
F♯m7 A/B D/E E/F♯

Medley options: Rise Up And Praise Him; Jesus Is Alive.

I will praise you, O Lord my God, with all my heart.... Psalm 86:12 (NIV)

I Give You My Heart

Words and Music by
REUBEN MORGAN

I wor-ship You.
E
D
A
Bsus
17
All I have with-in me, I give You
E
B/D♯
C♯m
A/E
E
21
praise, all that I a-dore is in You.
B/D♯
C♯m7
B/D♯
E
D
A
A/B

CHORUS
1st time - Solo
2nd & 3rd times - All
Lord, I give You my heart, I give You my soul, I
E
B
F♯m11
29
live for You a - lone. Eve - ry breath that I take,
A/B
E
eve - ry mo - ment I'm a - wake, Lord,
B/D♯
F♯m11
32
1
have Your way in me.
A/B
Amaj7
B/A
A/B

2
36
CHORUS
Melody - Middle Note
have Your way in me.
Lord, I give You my heart,
A/B
E
I give You my soul,
I live for You a-lone.
B
F♯m11
A/B
40
Eve-ry breath that I take,
eve-ry mo-ment I'm a-wake,
E
B/D♯
44
Lord, have Your way in me.
F♯m11
A/B
Amaj7

Soloist ad libs
B/A
G♯m7
C♯m7
8
Lord, I give You my heart,
I give You my soul.
Amaj7
B/A
52
Lord, I give You my heart,
G♯m7
C♯m7
C♯m7/B
Amaj7
I give You my soul.
B/A
G♯m7
C♯m7
C♯m7/B

56
Lord, I give You my heart, I give You my soul.
Amaj7
B/A
D.S.
3
have Your way in me.
G♯m7
C♯m7
A/B
A/B
61
CHORUS
Melody - Middle Note
Lord, I give You my heart, I give You my soul,
E
B
I live for You a - lone.
F♯m11
A/B

Medley Options: Be Glorified; O God You Are My God (WRIGHT).

...I saw the LORD seated on a throne, high and exalted... Isaiah 6:1 NIV

I See the Lord

Words and Music by
CHRIS FALSON

17
1.
VERSE
Lord of lords.
I see the Lord
C 7sus
C
F2
F
C/E
21
seat-ed on the throne
ex - al - ted,
and the train of His robe
Gm7
F/A
B♭2
C 7sus
C
F
C/E
25
fills the tem - ple with glo - ry,
and the whole earth is filled,
Gm7
F/A
B♭
G/B
F/C
and the whole earth is filled,
and the
Gm7/C
Fmaj7/C
B♭/C

29
whole earth is filled with His glo - ry.
Dm7
F/A
B♭2
B♭m6
F2
2.
33
VERSE
I see the Lord seat - ed on the throne ex-
G
D/F♯
Am7
G
C2
37
al - ted, and the train of His robe fills the tem - ple with
D 7sus
D
G
D/F♯
Am7
G/B
41
glo - ry, and the whole earth is filled, and the
C
A/C♯
G/D
Am7/D

45
whole earth is filled, and the whole earth is filled
Gmaj7/D
C/D
Em7
G/B
49
3rd time - instruments only
with His glo - ry. Ho - ly,
C2
Cm6
G2
G/D
53
3rd time voices enter
ho - ly, ho - ly, ho - ly, ho - ly is the
Am7/D
Gmaj7/D
C/D
G/B
Em7
C
Am7
57
Lord; Ho - ly, ho - ly, ho - ly,
Dsus
D
Am7
D
G/D
Am7/D
Gmaj7/D

61
ho - ly,
ho - ly
C/D
Em7
G/B
1, 2
D.S.
is the Lord of lords.
C
Am7
D 7sus
D
G2
65
3
Slower
rit.
Lord of lords.
San - to,
D 7sus
D
D 7sus
G
69
san - to,
san - to,
san - to,
san - to

Medley Options: All Heaven Declares; Crown Him King Of Kings

You turned my wailing into dancing;
You removed my sackcloth and clothed me with joy... Psalm 30:11 NIV

I Still Have Joy

Words and Music by
RON KENOLY

13 CHORUS
1st time unison
2nd time parts
ev'-ry-thing he could do to con-quer my soul. I still have joy, I
Dm7 C/E F F/G C Em7
still have joy, af-ter all I've been through, I still have joy; I
F C F C/E D7 G
17
still have joy, I still have joy,
C Em7 F G Am
af - ter all I've been through, I still have joy.
Dm7 C/E
1
Dm7 F/G C

21
VERSE
2. Friends have left me, they've ques-tioned my faith, the
C Em7 F C
good I tried to do was thrown back in my face; The
F C/E D7 G
25
hurt and the pain brought tears to my eyes, but
C Em7 F G C
God has re-placed a bless - ing for ev'-ry tear that I've cried. I
F C/E Dm F/G

2
30
still have joy.
I
still have peace,
I
still have peace,
still have His love,
I
still have His love,
still have joy,
I
still have joy,
Dm7
C
D♭
Fm7
G♭
D♭
Af - ter all I've been through,
I
still have peace;
I
Af - ter all I've been through,
I
still have His love;
I
Af - ter all I've been through,
I
still have joy;
I
G♭
D♭/F
E♭7
A♭
34
still have peace,
I
still have peace,
still have His love,
I
still have His love,
still have joy,
I
still have joy,
D♭
Fm7
G♭
A♭
B♭m

Medley Options: Center Of My Joy; Who's There? God's There.

...You will fill me with joy in your presence. Acts 2:28 NIV

I Was Created

Words and Music by
BILLY FUNK and DARYN FUNK

3rd time - 3 part
1.
by Your Spir - it, I live to wor - ship You.
of Your pres - ence, Your light in me shines through.
B♭ B♭/F F B♭ Csus C F
14
2, 3.
W. L. & Men
CHORUS
Ladies
All
My heart's My heart's, on - ly de - sire (re) is to
F B♭/D C/E F F/A
W. L. & Men
19
Ladies
wor - ship You. My life, My life,
B♭ Csus C F B♭/D C/E
All
W. L. & Men
free - ly I give You, make it ho - ly, pure and true; My eyes
F F/A B♭ Dm Csus

23
Ladies
All
My eyes,
see with Your Spir - it when I fel - low-ship with You;
B♭/D
C/E
F
F/A
B♭
A/C♯
27
last time to Coda
I was cre-at - ed to live in Your pre - sence, Lord.
Dm
Gm7
F/A
B♭
Csus
C
1.
2.
F
Gm9
C 7sus
F

33
BRIDGE
All
Sure - ly good - ness and mer - cy follow me
Bb F/A Gm7 Csus C
all the days of my life, As I learn to yield
37
Praise Team
As I learn to yield
F F/A Bb Eb
39
D.S. al Coda
my heart to You; My heart's,
Men
my heart to You. My heart's,
Gm7 Csus C/Bb F/A

Medley options: Praise To The Lord.

1226

...Let us run with perseverance the race marked out for us. Hebrews 12:1 (NIV)

I Will Run To You

Words and Music by
DARLENE ZSCHECH

♩ = 80

Fm Eb Db Fm Eb Db

Bbm7 Cm7 Db Eb Db/Ab Eb/Ab Ab

Worship Leader

Your eye

10 *VERSE*

Db/Ab Eb/Ab Ab Db/Ab Eb/G

is on the spar - row, and Your hand, it com - forts me;

14
From the ends of the earth, to the depths of my heart, Let Your
Fm Fm/E♭ G♭/D♭ D♭ E♭ E♭/G A♭ A♭2/C
18
mer - cy and strength be seen; You call me to Your pur -
D♭ B♭m7 E♭sus E♭ D♭ E♭
pose As an - gels un - der - stand, For Your glo -
A♭ D♭ Fm Fm/E♭
22
ry may You draw all men as Your love and grace de - mands.
G♭/D♭ D♭ E♭ E♭/G A♭ A♭/C D♭ E♭

1st time - Worship Leader only
2nd & 3rd time - All
26
CHORUS
And I will run to You, To Your words
A♭
D♭/A♭
E♭/G
A♭
of truth, not by might, not by pow -
E♭/G
C/E
Fm
Fm/E♭
B♭m7
Worship Leader
30
2nd & 3rd time - All
er, but by the Spir - it of God; Yes, I will run
A♭/C
D♭
B♭/D
E♭
A♭
34
the race 'Til I see Your face;
D♭/A♭
E♭/G
A♭
E♭/G
C/E

38
O, let me live in the glo - ry of Your grace.
Fm
Fm/E♭
B♭m7
A♭/C
E♭
1.
2.
D.S.
You call
And I will run
D♭/A♭
E♭/A♭
A♭
A♭
3.
Worship Leader
45
CHORUS
And I will run to You,
A♭
D♭/A♭
E♭/A♭
To Your words of truth,
See, it's not by might,
A♭
E♭/G
C/E
Fm
Fm/E♭

50
not by pow - er, but by the Spir - it of God;
Bbm7
Ab/C
Db
Bb/D
All
54
Yes, I will run the race
Eb
Eb/G
F/A
'Til I see Your face;
O, let me live
Bb
F/A
D/F#
Gm
Gm/F
58
in the glo - ry of Your grace.
Cm7
Bb/D
F
Eb/Bb
F/Bb

62
And I will run to You, To Your words
B♭ E♭/B♭ F/A B♭
Worship Leader
66
of truth, See, it's not by might, not by pow -
F/A D/F♯ Gm Gm/F Cm7
All
er, but by the Spir - it of God; Yes, I will run
B♭/D E♭ C/E F B♭
70
the race 'Til I see Your face;
E♭/B♭ F/A B♭ F/A D/F♯

74
Worship Leader
O, let me live in the glo - ry, O, let me live
Gm
Gm/F
Cm7
B♭/D
All
78
in the glo - ry, please, let me live in the glo -
E♭
B♭/F
Cm7
Worship Leader
All
ry of Your grace.
And I will run
B♭/D
F 7sus
E♭/B♭
B♭
E♭/B♭
82
Worship Leader
All
to You,
And I will run to You,
Fsus/B♭
B♭
E♭/A♭
Fsus/A♭
B♭/A♭

Medley options: Power Of Your Love; All Heaven Declares.

1227

The eternal God is your refuge, and underneath are the everlasting arms.... Deuteronomy 33:27 (NIV)

In The Arms Of His Love

Words and Music by
CARL and LEANN ALBRECHT

3rd time - Duet with Background Vocals
Melody - Bottom Note
Noth - ing can harm me, no rea - son to fear;
Dm7
C/E
E/G♯
Am7
11
1
2, 3
Safe in the arms of His love.
In the love.
Safe in the arms.
Dm7
Gsus
G
C
Gsus
G
C
G/B
VERSE
14
Solo
Soft - ly He speaks to my spir - it,
Am
C/G
F
C/E

Duet
Melody - Bottom Note
draw - ing me in - to His grace;
Dm7 C/E Bb(add2) Gsus G
18
Solo
Lay - ing a - side all my wor - ries and pride, to
Am7 Dsus D
Duet
Melody - Bottom Note
last time to Coda
en - ter His gen - tle em - brace. In the
Dm7 C/E Bb(add2) Gsus G
22
Coda
Instrumental
brace.
Bb(add2) G/A A D D/F# G G/A

D
D/F♯
26
G
D/F♯
Em7
D/F♯
Duet
Melody - Bottom Note
Safe in the arms of Your
F♯/A♯
Bm7
Em7
Asus
A
30
CHORUS
All
Solo
love.
In the arms of Your love, I find
In the arms of Your love;
D
G/A A G/A A
D
D/F♯

Duet with Background Vocals
Melody - Bottom Note
rest; In the arms of Your love, there's sweet
In the arms of Your love;
G G/A A D D/F♯
34
qui - et - ness; Noth - ing can harm me, no
A/G G D/F♯ Em7 D/F♯
rea - son to fear; Safe in the arms of Your
Safe in the arms.
F♯/A♯ Bm7 Em7 Asus A

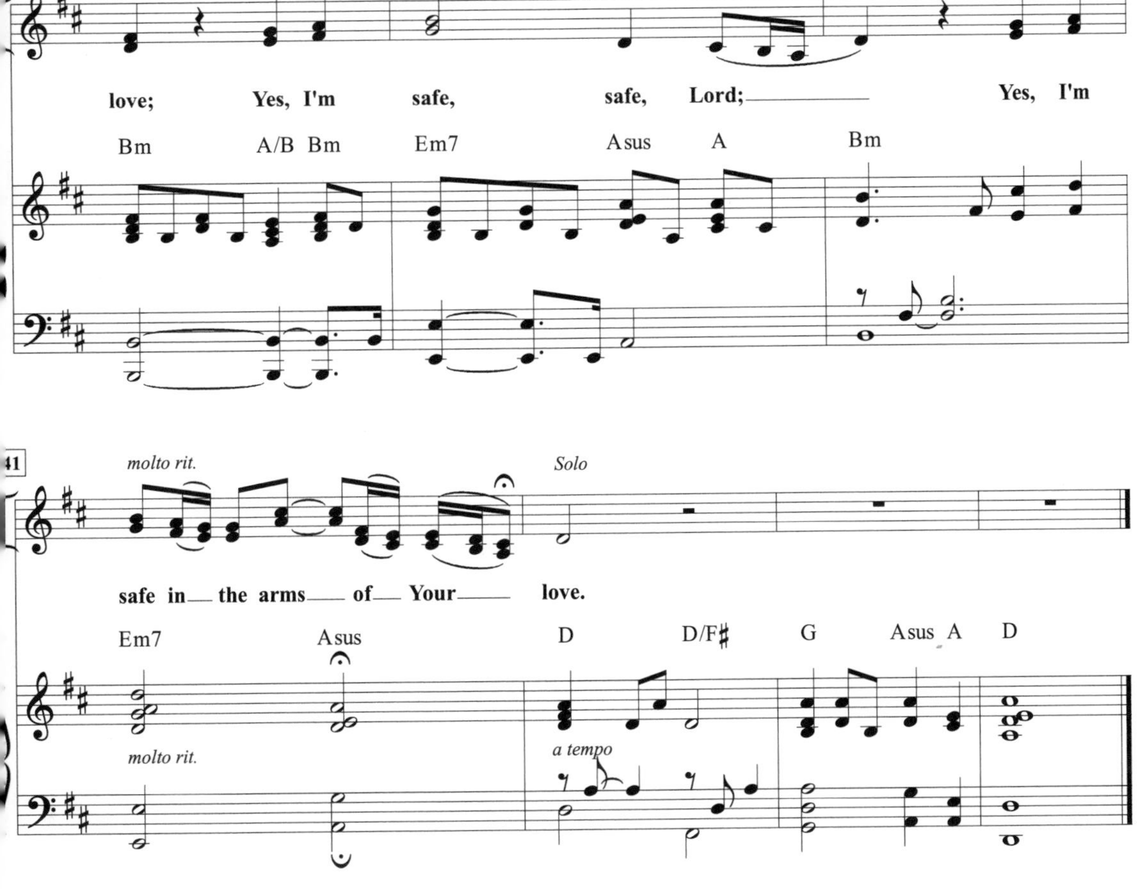

Medley Options: Like A Shepherd; No Eye Has Seen (BALOCHE/KERR).

It is good to praise the LORD
and make music to Your name, O Most High... Psalm 92:1 NIV

It Is Good

Words and Music by
DAN ADLER

13
sing of Your faith - ful - ness and lov - ing kind - ness both day and night;
F
B♭
Gm7
C11
F
B♭
17
To play on our in - stru - ments sweet songs of praise for the
F/C Dm
Gm7 C
F
B♭
Gm7
C11
21
things You do,
It is good, it is good, it is
F
B♭
Gm7
B♭/C
C11
F
B♭
4th time to Coda
1, 2
good to give thanks to You.
Gm7
C11
F
B♭
Gm7
C
F

VERSE
Worship Leader
25
For though the wick - ed spring up like the grass and are ev' - ry - where,
For though we strug - gle and tri - als and trou - bles still come our way,
Bb C Dm C F Bb
All
29
soon they will van - ish; but all those plant - ed in Your house will grow with - out
You won't for - sake - us; Your Word has told us Your prom - is - es will nev - er
F Dm C Bb C Dm Gm7
end.
end.
Sing it a - gain! It is You.
C Bb/D C/E C F Bb Gm7 C F
BRIDGE
35
Worship Leader
Congregation
Why give Him praise? Be - cause He is wor - thy.
F Bb C F

W.L.
Cong.
Why should we sing? He loves you and me.
B♭
C/E
C
F
39
W.L.
Cong.
Why give Him thanks? Be - cause He for-gave us.
W.L.
Cong.
Why cel - e-brate? Be -
B♭
C
F
B♭
W.L.
43
Cong.
cause we are free. And when should we thank Him? In
C/E
C
F
F
B♭
W.L.
Cong.
morn - ing and eve - ning. In what cir - cum-stance? The
C
Dm
F
B♭

W.L.
47
Cong.
good and the bad. Is it al - ways eas - y? No,
C/E C F B♭
W.L.
All
it's not so eas - y. But is it good? Yes, it's
C Dm F B♭
50
D.S. al Coda
good, it is good, it is good. It is
C B♭/D C/E C11
Coda
55
You. It is good, it is good, it is
F B♭ Gm7 C F B♭

Medley Options: Celebrate The Lord Of Love; Mourning Into Dancing

1229

...You shall worship the LORD your God, and Him only shall you serve. Luke 4:8 NKJ

It's Only You, Jesus

Words and Music by
JAMIE HARVILL

Worship Leader
10
You; There's a hole in my heart that on-ly You can fill, and
E B/E E B/E E B/E
though my eyes may wan-der, You draw me back 'cause still, it's on-ly
E B/E E B/E
14
It's on-ly You.
2nd time - Praise team
You, Je - sus, You,
E/A B/A F♯m7(add4) E B/E
All
18
CHORUS
You. With Your stead - fast love You touch
E B/E B

my heart and You move me,
and I
A
E
B/E
E
22
mar-vel at the way that You pur-sue me.
B
F♯m7(add4)
E
B/E
26
Worship Leader
The on-ly thing that I can do is to bring
Praise Team
Ooo,
E
C♯m
G♯/B♯

30
All
You praise because it's due to no one else but You,
Ooo;
E/B
F♯/A♯
F♯m7(add4)
Worship Leader
All
W. L.
only You, You, only
B 7sus
E
B/E
E
B/E
34
All
last time to Coda
W. L.
1.
All
You, Jesus; Only You,
E/A
B/A
A
E
B/E

W. L.
38
All
W. L.
You, on - ly You, Je - sus. There is
E B/E E/A B/A A
2.
All
W. L.
You, You, on - ly
C♯m7 E/B
42
All
D.S. al Coda
You, Je - sus. With Your
E/A B/A A
44
Coda
All
W. L.
46
All
W. L.
On - ly You, on - ly You, on - ly
E B/E E B/E

All
W. L.
49
You, Je - sus. The on - ly thing that I
Praise Team
Ooo,
E/A
B/A
A
C♯m
50
can do is to bring You praise be - cause it's due
Ooo;
G♯/B♯
E/B
F♯/A♯
54
All
Worship Leader
to no one else but You, on - ly
F♯m7(add4)
B 7sus

Medley options: Jesus, Jesus; Open The Eyes Of My Heart.

Let us fix our eyes on Jesus, the author and perfecter of our faith.... Hebrews 12:2 NIV

Jesus

12
He rose a - gain, He rose a -
Db2 Ebm7 Db2/F Gbmaj7 Ab Db2/F Gbmaj7 Gb6
16
gain, He rose, He rose,
Db2/Ab Eb/G F/A Bbm Ab6 Fm7 Ebm7 Ab9 Bbm7 Fm7
20
He rose a - gain. He reigns on
Ebm7 Db/F Gbmaj7 Ab F#m7 Amaj7 Amaj7/C# B E C#m F#m7 B
high, He reigns on high,
E E/D# C#m B11 B/A E2/G# Amaj7 A6 E2/G# C#m7 D#m7 G#7

24
He reigns, He reigns, He reigns on
C♯m B6 F♯m7 C♯m7 G♯m7 F♯m7 E/G♯ Amaj7 B
28
high. For - ev - er - more,
F♯m7 E/G♯ A B/D♯ E F♯m7 G♯7 C♯m Emaj7/B Amaj7 B/A
32
for - ev - er - more, He reigns,
G♯m7 C♯m7 F♯m7 Amaj7 G2 Cmaj7 F♯m7 B Amaj7 G♯m7
He reigns for - ev - er - more.
F♯m7 C♯m7 G♯m7 F♯m7 Amaj7/C♯ B/D♯ E Gm7/C C11

Medley options: My Redeemer Lives (GRECO); Jesus Lord To Me

Jesus said to him, "I am the way, the truth, and the life. No one comes to the Father except through Me." John 14:6 NKJ

Jesus Is The Way

Words and Music by
MARK CONDON

14
time you need - ed a Sav - ior
clue what a Sav - ior
G7(♭5 ♭9)
Fmaj9
C2/E
18
to give you peace, peace of mind? Do you re-mem -
like my God could do? He said if
Dm11
Dm7/G
Cmaj9
ber what shape your life was in? Well,
they would just call up - on His name, He would
Gm9
B♭/C

22
Je - sus is still the an - swer, He can
hear their hum - ble cry and de -
Dm11
C2/E
do it all o - ver a - gain.
liv - er them to - day.
Fmaj7
Dm7/G
G13
27
CHORUS
W.L.
He's the on - ly, on - ly way;
Praise Team
Je - sus is the way,
C2
Gm7

31
He never changes;
He's the only way;
C9
Fmaj7
C2/E
35
He never changes, He's still the same;
Jesus
Dm11
Fmaj7/G
C2
He's the only, only way;
is the way,
He's the only
Gm7
C9

39
way;
Je - sus is still the an -
Fmaj7
C2/E
Dm11
1.
44
swer for to - day.
Fmaj7/G
A♭maj9
B♭2
2.
C2
C/B♭

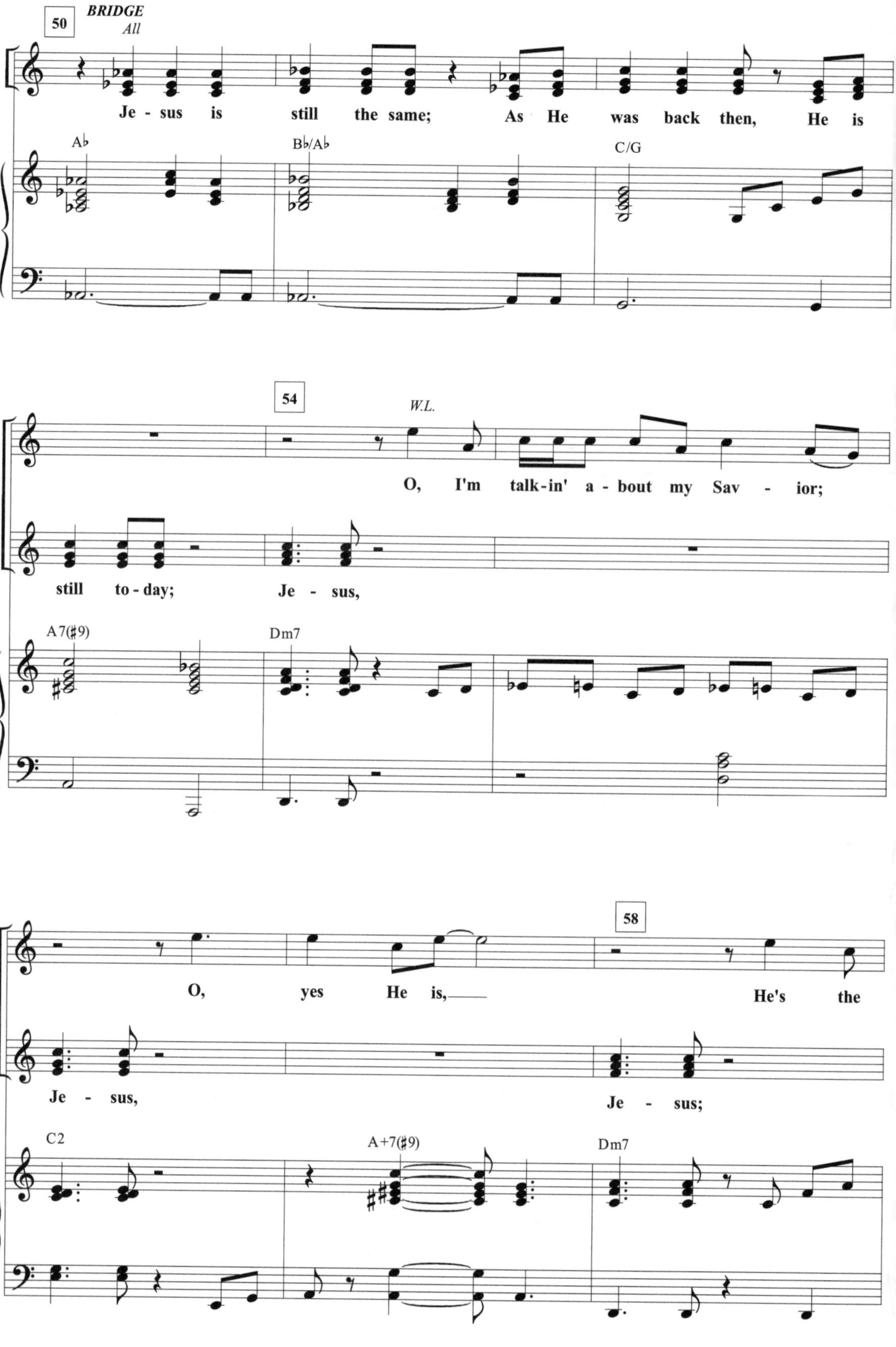
50
BRIDGE
All
Je - sus is still the same; As He was back then, He is
Ab
Bb/Ab
C/G
54
W.L.
O, I'm talk-in' a - bout my Sav - ior;
still to - day; Je - sus,
A7(#9)
Dm7
O, yes He is,
58
He's the
Je - sus, Je - sus;
C2
A+7(#9)
Dm7

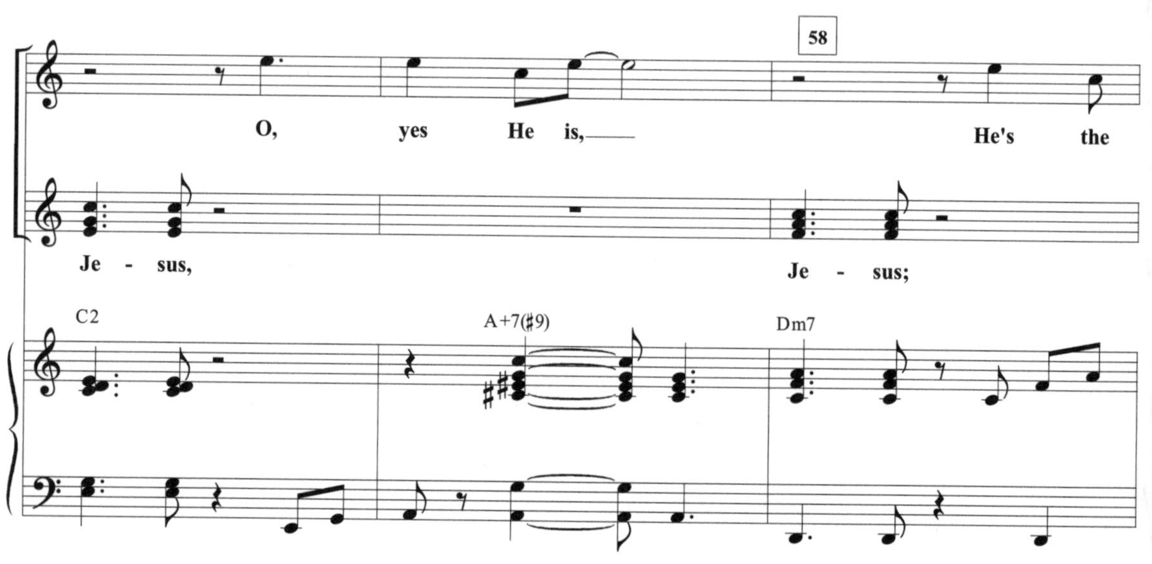

on - ly way.
He's the on - ly way.
Fmaj7/G
Dm7/G
C
G♭/A♭
A♭
62 CHORUS
He's the on - ly, on - ly way;
Je - sus is the way,
D♭
A♭m7
66
He nev - er chang - es;
He's the on - ly way;
D♭9
G♭maj7
D♭2/F

70
He nev - er chang - es, He's still the same;
Je - sus
E♭m11
G♭maj7/A♭
D♭2
He's the on - ly, on - ly way;
is the way,
He's the on - ly
A♭m7
D♭9
74
way;
Je - sus is still the an -
G♭maj7
D♭2/F
E♭m11

78
swer for to - day.
G♭maj7/A♭
D♭
A♭/B♭
B♭m7
80
BRIDGE
81
Tenors - 2nd time only
He nev-er chang - es,
Altos
Je-sus Christ is still the same;
Je-sus Christ is still
E♭m11
D♭2/F
84
He nev-er chang - es;
He nev-er chang -
the same,
Je-sus Christ is still the same,
G♭maj9

1.
1st time - Tenors enter
es,
He nev-er chang - es;
Je-sus Christ is still the same,
Je-sus Christ is still
D♭2/F
B♭m7
E♭m11
2.
Sopranos
90
The Lord is here,
He nev - er chang - es,
Tenors
Altos
the same,
Je - sus Christ is still
B♭m7
E♭m11
here for you;
He nev - er chang - es;
the same;
Je - sus Christ is still
D♭2/F

94
The Lord is here,
He nev - er chang - es,
the same,
Je - sus Christ is still
Gbmaj9
here for you;
He nev - er chang - es,
the same,
Je - sus Christ is still
Db2/F
98
The Lord is here,
He nev - er chang - es,
the same,
Bbm7
Ebm11

102

Molto ritard

here for you.

G♭maj9

G♭/A♭

D♭2

Medley options: Center Of My Joy.

Shout! For the LORD has given you the city! Joshua 6:16 NIV

Joshua Generation

Words and Music by
RON KENOLY

19
'til ev'-ry bat-tle is won; We're the Josh-u-a gen-er-a-
Em7sus
A7(♯9)
Dm
C
tion, a cho-sen and a-noint-ed na-tion,
Dm
Gm7
23
3rd time to Coda
Jer-i-cho knows we are com-ing, and the walls of Jer-i-cho are com-ing
Dm/A
G/A
Dm/A
Gm7
Am7
Dm
1
27
VERSE
Worship Leader
down. 1. They heard a-bout the plagues of E-gypt and how the
Dm

31
peo - ple of the Lord were set free; They heard a - bout Pha-roah's ar -
B♭/D
C/D
Dm
C
my and how they drowned in the Red Sea; They
Dm
Em7sus
Am7
35
heard a - bout the cloud that led by day and the fire in the sky each
Dm
C
Dm
Gm7
39
night; They know that our God is with us and they know
Dm/A
G/A
Dm/A
Gm7

VERSE
Worship Leader
2
– that we know how to fight.
down.
2. They
A7(♯9)
Dm
44
heard a-bout our wil-der-ness ex - per-i-ence and how the old and the fear - ful passed a-
Dm
B♭/D
C/D
48
way;
They heard that we crossed o-ver Jor - dan, we're get-ting
Dm
C
Dm
52
clos-er and clos - er ev'-ry day;
With the high-er prais - es of God
Em7sus
A7(♯9)
Dm

in our mouths and a two - edged sword in our hand, they
Dm
Gm7
56
know that our God is with us and we're com-ing to pos-sess the
Dm/A
G/A
Dm/A
Gm7
Am7
Dm
60
land.
B♭/D
C/D
D.S. al Coda
B♭maj7/D
C/D
B♭/D
C/E
Am7
C
Dm

Coda
67
BRIDGE
down.
Down, down, down, the walls
Dm
Dm C/D Dm
71
of Jer - i - cho are com - ing down;
Down, down, down,
Gm Am Dm Dm
ev - 'ry strong - hold will be lev - eled to the ground. We're the
Em A
75
Josh - u - a gen - er - a - tion, a cho - sen and a - noint - ed na -
Dm C Dm Gm7

Medley Options: We Are Possessing; God Has Given Us The City

He is the God who avenges me.... who sets me free from my enemies.... 2 Sam. 22:48-49 NIV

Jubilee

Words and Music by
TOM BYNUM

Congregation
sing - ing and danc - ing for you and me;
G C G C
15 Worship Leader
Thank - ing and prais - ing be - cause we're free,
G C G C
Congregation
thank-ing and prais-ing be - cause we're free; O,
19 Worship Leader
this is the year of
G C G C G C
Ju - bi-lee,
Congregation
O, this is the year of Ju - bi - lee.
Worship Leader
Put your hands to -
G C G C G C

23
geth - er,
ev'-ry-bod-y praise the Lord,
G
C
27
put your hands to - geth - er,
sing and shout and praise the Lord.
1
O yeah!
Fmaj7
Em7
D11
2
All
32
VERSE
Ev'-ry - thing that was sto-len shall be re - turned un-to me,
E11
E
N.C.

Moth - er, fa - ther, sis - ter, broth - er, they will all go free; Ev'-ry -
36
thing that was sto - len shall be re - turned un - to me,
Am
Em/B
Am/C
Em
40
sing-ing, danc-ing, prais-ing, shout-ing, in - crease and vic-to - ry.
Am
Em/B
D11
G
C
Ev'-ry -
G
C
G
C
G
E11
E

44
VERSE
thing that was sto-len shall be re - turned un-to me,
Moth-er, fa-ther, sis-ter, broth-er,
Am7 N.C.
48
they will all go free; Ev'-ry - thing that was sto - len shall be re - turned un-to me,
52
sing-ing, danc-ing, prais-ing, shout-ing, in - crease and vic-to - ry.
D11
N.C.
55
Dm7 Fmaj7 G
gliss.
G C

D G C Am D G C D Em

63 *VERSE*

Ev'-ry - thing that was sto - len shall be re -

A7 Am7 D Bm7 E N.C.

turned un - to me, Moth - er, fa - ther, sis - ter, broth - er,

67

they will all___ go free; Ev'-ry - thing that was sto - len shall be re -

Am7 D G/B

Medley Options: I Will Dance; Mourning Into Dancing

Teach me your way, O Lord; lead me in a straight path. Psalm 27:11 (NIV)

Lead Me

Words and Music by
CRAIG SMITH

will speak before I say one single word;
where I go, Your presence will be there with me;
G/D
F2
G
13
W.L. & Men
You know my deep thoughts, all that I treasure,
All
You knew me before birth, laid out each moment,
D5
G/D
D5
17
You skillfully guide me,
You've planned ev'ry day for me,
G/D
D5
G/D

21
CHORUS
1st time W.L. only, bottom note
2nd & 3rd times, P.T. Men add top note
make me know Your will. Fa-ther, lead me
Praise Team
guide me in Your will. Fa - ther, lead
F
A
Em7
D/F♯
G
a-way from the things of the world; Fa-ther, lead
me; Oo;
A
Em7
D/F♯
G
A
25
me by Your truth and the light of Your Word;
Fa - ther, lead me; Oo;
Em7
D/F♯
G
A
Em7
D/F♯
G

29
Fa - ther, lead me,
Fa - ther, lead me.
A
Em7
D/F♯
G
A
last time to Coda
33
search my heart and lead me in Your way.
E
D/F♯
G2
D5
1.
G/D
D5
G/D

Medley options: Prepare the Way.

Sing to the LORD! Give praise to the LORD!... Jeremiah 20:13 NIV

Let Us Come Into This House

Words and Music by
MARK CONDON

11
O, let ev - 'ry - bod - y lift their voice
Am7 G/B Am/D G/C G/B G/D
15
un - to the Lord;
For He's been so might - y good
D Cmaj7 G2/B
to you and He keeps on bless - ing and bless - ing you; So, give
Am9 E+7(♯9)
19
prais - es, high prais - es;
Am7 G/B

23
last time to Coda
Let some - bod - y give praise un - to the Lord.
E+7(♯9)
E+7(♭9)
Am7
G/D
Am11/D
G
1.
Ladies
2.
Some - bod - y give
N.C.
N.C.
29
VERSE
Worship Leader
I'm stand - ing here to - day be - cause of what my God has done;
Cmaj9
G2/B
Am7
C/D
G
33
I'm a liv - ing wit - ness of how the
Cmaj9
G2/B

37
Lord can change some - one;
You see, ev - er - y day
Am7
C/D
G
D/F♯
Em
He keeps bless - ing me in a brand new way;
Baug/D♯
G/D
Em/C♯
41
I can't keep it to my - self, I got - ta tell some - bod - y to - day.
Am7
G/D
C
C/D
Ladies
D.S. al Coda
Some - bod - y give

Medley options: How Good It Is; Sing, Shout, Clap.

Your kingdom come. Your will be done on earth as it is in heaven. Matthew 6:10 (NKJ)

Let Your Kingdom Come

Words and Music by
CRAIG SMITH

9
Christ our King rules o - ver all, and
You a - lone reign sov - 'reign - ly,
throne re - mains e - ter - nal - ly;
o; You
D A E F♯m
1.
13
You will reign for - ev - er.
You will reign for - ev -
You will reign for - ev -
will reign for - ev -
D A E F♯m D A
E A

2, 3.
18
er,
our
God
reigns
for - ev -
P.T. 3rd time only
er,
our
God
reigns
for - ev -
E
F♯m
D
A
er.
All
Let Your king - dom
come,
er.
E
A
Bm
E
22
CHORUS
let Your will be
done,
let Your king - dom
come;
E
F♯m
D
Bm
A

26
Let Your king-dom come, let Your will be done, let Your king-dom come.
Bm
E
F♯m
D
Bm
A
1.
2.
A
Let Your king-dom come,
Bm
E
31
CHORUS
let Your will be done, let Your king-dom come;
F♯m
D
Bm
A
35
Let Your king-dom come, let Your will be done, let Your king-dom come.
Bm
E
F♯m
D
Bm
A

BRIDGE All
39
One God, one
A
C2
Lord, one King, one Ma - jes - ty;
Praise Team
Whoa;
D
G
A
43
W.L. One High, one Lift - ed Up,
All
one Ho - ly Pow'r.
C2
D
G
48
Esus
D
A

E
F♯m
D
A
E
52
1st time W.L. only
God reigns,
God reigns forever;
Praise Team on repeat
God reigns,
God reigns;
D
A
E
F♯m
D
A
56
er;
God reigns,
God reigns,
E
D
A
E
F♯m

1.
2.
God reigns for - ev - er.
er.
God reigns.
D
A
E
E
61
D
A
E
F♯m
D
A
65
Our God reigns,
our
Our God reigns,
our
E
D
A
E
F♯m

1, 2, 3.
68
God reigns for-ev - er. Our
God reigns for-ev - er. Our God reigns.
4.
D
A
E
D
A
All
72
CHORUS
Let Your king-dom come, let Your will be done,
E
Bm
E
F♯m
D
let Your king-dom come;
1, 2.
Let Your king-dom come,
Bm
A
Bm
E

Medley options: For The Lord Is Good (DeSHAZO/SADLER); There's A New Generation.

1237

Great is the LORD and most worthy of praise... Psalm 145:3 NIV

Lord, You're Worthy

Words and Music by
MARK CONDON

15
Lord, I love You,
Db♭m6/A♭
A♭2
I a - dore You;
19
Lord, You're wor - thy for al - ways.
E♭/A♭
D♭/A♭
1.
D♭/E♭
A♭
D♭/E♭
2.
24 CHORUS
Lord, You're wor -
G♭2
D♭/E♭
A♭2

W.L. ad libs
thy,
Lord, You're wor - thy;
Eb/Ab
28
Ebm7/Ab
Lord, You're wor - thy of our praise;
Db/Ab
Dbm6/Ab
32
Ab2
Lord, I love You,
I a - dore You;
36
Eb/Ab
Db/Ab
Lord, You're wor -

38
1.
2. All - Ladies sing melody
thy for al - ways.
So we
Db/Eb
Ab
Db/Eb
Gb/Ab
41
BRIDGE
W.L. ad libs
praise
You,
we
praise
Dbmaj9
Ab2/C
45
You;
We
praise
You
Fm7
Bbm11
Bbm11/Eb
Bbm7/Eb
49
for Your awe - some might - y ways;
We
praise
Gb/Ab
D9(b5)
Dbmaj9

You, we praise You;
A♭2/C
Fm7
53
1.
Lord, You're wor thy of our praise.
B♭m7
D♭/E♭
A♭
2.
So we praise;
G♭/A♭
A♭
Fm7
59
Lord, You're wor thy of our praise;
B♭m7
D♭/E♭
A♭2

Medley options: All Of Our Praise.

1238

Oh, sing to the LORD a new song! For He has done marvelous things... Psalm 98:1 NKJ

Marvelous Things

Words and Music by
MARK CONDON

14
All
all that He has done; Let us mag-ni-fy the King of all kings; He has
G13
Dm9
G13
1.
2.
W.L.
done man - y mar-vel - ous things. Give Him things. We have
Em7(♭5)
A7(♭9)
Dm7
Aaug7
N.C.
19
VERSE
come in - to this house to praise the Lord, let us lift up our voice and
Dm9
G13
Dm9
23
sing; In one mind and one ac-cord, let us wor-ship the Lord, for He's
A13(♭9,♯11)
Dm9
G13

All
3.
W.L.
done man-y mar - vel-ous things. Hey! Give Him things. O, there'll
Em7(♭5) A7(♭9) Dm9 Aaug7 N.C.
28
nev-er be a stone that-'ll cry out in my place, I'm here to give God the
Dm9 G13 Dm9
32
praise; You see, ev-'ry-thing in me, just has to shout and sing
A13(♭9,♯11) Dm9 G13
All
of His man-y mar - vel-ous ways. Hey! Give Him
Em7(♭5) A7(♭9) Dm9 Aaug7

36
CHORUS
W.L.
All
W.L.
glo - ry, to the Ho - ly One; Give Him hon - or, for
Dm9
G13
Dm9
All
40
3
all that He has done; Let us mag - ni - fy the King of all kings; He has
G13
Dm9
G13
done man - y mar - vel - ous things. Let us
Em7(♭5)
A7(♭9)
N.C.
44
BRIDGE
praise Him in the morn - ing, praise Him all night long; Give
D/A
A/G

3
praise in ev - e - ry - thing; Let us
D/F♯
Em D Em7(♭5)
3
3
48
praise Him in the morn - ing, praise Him all night long,
D/A
A/G
1.
2.
Sopranos
for His mar - vel - ous things. Give Him things. Let us
Em7 G/A D Aaug7 D
53
BRIDGE
praise Him in the morn - ing, praise Him all night long; Give
D/A
A/G

Altos
praise in ev - e - ry - thing; Let us
D/F♯
Em
D
Em7(♭5)
D/F♯
Gmin6
Em7(♭5)
3
57
praise Him in the morn - ing, praise Him all night long; Give
D/A
A/G
Tenors
praise in ev - er - y - thing; Let us
61
praise Him in the morn - ing, praise Him all night long; Give

All
praise in ev - er - y - thing; Let us
D/F♯ Em D Em7(♭5) D/F♯ Gmin6 Em7(♭5)
65
praise Him in the morn - ing, praise Him all night long; Give
D/A A/G
praise in ev - er - y - thing; Let us
D/F♯ Em D Em7(♭5) D/F♯ Gmin6 Em7(♭5)
69
praise Him in the morn - ing, praise Him all night long,
D/A A/G

last time to Coda
for His mar - vel - ous things.
Em7
G/A
D
75
BRIDGE
Let us praise Him in the morn - ing,
D/A
praise Him all night long; Give praise in ev - e - ry -
A/G
D/F♯
Em D
3
79
thing; Let us praise Him in the morn - ing, praise Him all night long,
Em7(♭5)
D/A
A/G

Medley options: One Of Us.

The Great, the Mighty God, whose name *is* the LORD of hosts. Jeremiah 32:18 NKJV

Mighty God

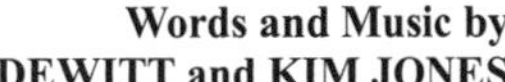
Words and Music by
DEWITT and KIM JONES

♩ = 108

13
Might-y God, might-y God, yes, You are might-y God.
Fm/D
D♭13(♯11)
G(♯9♭13)
C(♯9♭13)
Fm
B♭/F
A♭/F
1
You are a
2
Worship Leader
You are
18
might - y, You are might - y; Might-y
All
Fm7
Fm9
Fm6
22
God, might-y God, yes, You are might - y God.
D♭13(♯11)
G(♯9♭13)
C(♯9♭13)
Fm
1

Worship Leader
You are God.
You are a
Fm
Bb/F
Ab/F
Fm
A/C♯
ho - ly God,
You are a ho - ly God,
F♯m7sus
F♯m7sus
32
Ho - ly God, ho - ly God, yes, You are ho - ly
F♯m/D♯
D13(♯11)
G♯(♯9b13)
C♯(♯9b13)
God.
You are a
Worship Leader
37
You are ho - ly,
F♯m
B/F♯
A/F♯
F♯m
F♯m
F♯m7

All
41
You are ho - ly, Ho-ly God, ho-ly God, yes,
F♯m9
F♯m6
D13(♯11)
Worship Leader
1
2
You are ho-ly God.
You are God.
G♯(♯9♭13)
C♯(♯9♭13)
F♯m
F♯m
46
F♯m7sus
F♯m7sus
F♯m/D♯
50
D13(♯11)
G♯(♯9♭13)
C♯(♯9♭13)
F♯m
B/F♯
A/F♯

54
You are an awe - some God,
You are an
F♯m B♭/D
Gm7sus
58
awe - some God,
Awe-some God, awe-some God, yes,
Gm7sus
Gm/E
E♭13(♯11)
You are awe-some God.
You are an
A(♯9♭13)
D(♯9♭13)
Gm
C/G B♭/G
Gm
Gm
gliss
1
2
63
67
Awe-some God, awe-some God, yes,
N.C.
Fsus/B♭ Csus/F Dsus/E
E♭13(♯9)

W.L. You are awe -
– You are awe - some God.
A(♯9♭13)
D(♯9♭13)
Gm
C/G
B♭/G
Gm

some, You are awe - some.
71
All
P.T. Ah awe - some God, Awe - some
N.C.
Fsus/B♭
Csus/F
Dsus/E

75
God, awe-some God, yes, You are awe-some God.
E♭13(♯9)
A(♯9♭13)
D(♯9♭13)
Gm
C/G
B♭/G
Gm

79
Gm
C/G
B♭/G
Gm
C/G
B♭/G
Gm
C/G
B♭/G
Gm
B♭
A
A♭

83
You are might - y, You are might - y God, You are ho - ly,
Gm C/G B♭/G Gm C/G B♭/G Gm C/G B♭/G
87
You are ho - ly God. Might - y, might - y, might - y, ho - ly, ho - ly, ho - ly,
Gm B♭ A A♭ Gm C/G Gm C/G Gm Gm C/G Gm C/G Gm
91
Might - y, might - y, might - y, ho - ly, ho - ly, ho - ly, Ah
Gm C/G Gm C/G Gm Gm C/G Gm C/G Gm N.C.
awe - some God.
Fsus/B♭ Csus/F Gm
sfz

1240

Search me, O God, and know my heart.... Psalm 139:23 (NIV)

My Heart, Your Home

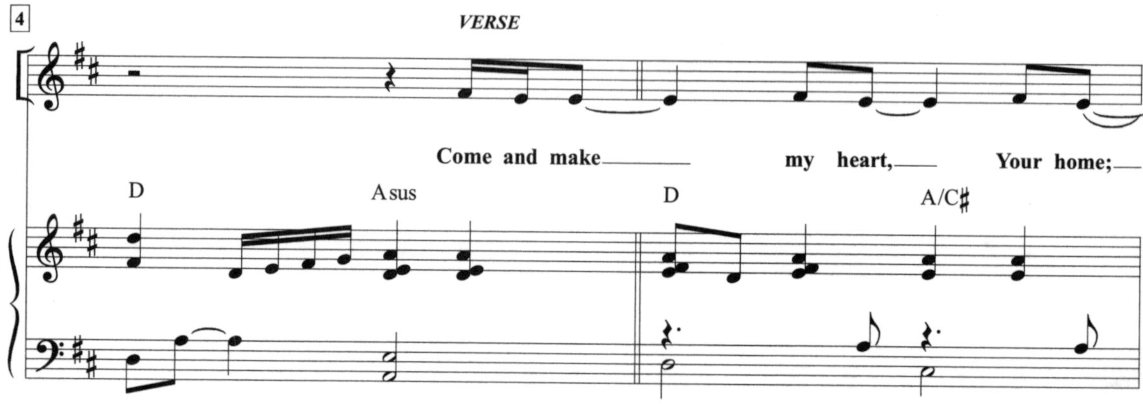

9
know.
Search me through and through,
Asus
A
D
A/C♯
till my heart be-comes a home for You.
Bm7
D/A
Gmaj7
A/C♯
VERSE
13
Come and make my heart, Your home;
D
Asus
D
A/C♯
Come and be eve-ry-thing I am and all I
Bm7
D/A
G
D/F♯

17
know.
Search me through and through,
Asus
A
D
A/C♯
till my heart be-comes a home for You.
Bm7
D/A
Gmaj7
A/C♯
CHORUS
1st time - Melody (Middle note) and Alto (Bottom note)
2nd time - 3 parts
20
A home for You,
oh;
A home for You,
D
D/F♯
G
A/C♯
D
D/F♯
23
oh,
oh;
Let eve - ry - thing I
G
A
Bm

27
VERSE
Melody - Middle Note
31
_ do, _ o-pen up _ a door _ for You _ to come _ through; Then
my heart would _ be _ a place where You wan-na be. Come and make _
_ my heart, _ Your home; _ Come and be
eve-ry-thing _ I _ am and all _ I _ know. _
C
G/B
Asus
D
A/C♯
Bm
D/A
G
D/F♯
Asus
A

Search me through and through, till my heart be-comes
D
A/C♯
Bm7
D/A
35
1
a home for You. A home for You,
Gmaj7
A/C♯
D
D/F♯
2
Till my heart be-comes a home for You;
D
Bm7
Gmaj7
A
39
Till my heart be-comes a home
Bm7
D/F♯
G
Asus

Medley Options: Bowing My Heart; Turn My Heart.

I know that my Redeemer lives.... Job 19:25 (NIV)

My Redeemer Lives

Words and Music by
REUBEN MORGAN

13
My shame He's
E7
A7
E7
tak-en a-way,
my pain is healed in His name,
I be-lieve,
A7
E7
A7
7
I be-lieve.
E7
A7
E7
21
Unison
Parts
I'll raise a ban - ner,
'cause my Lord has
A7
Bsus
A(no5)

CHORUS
25
con-quered the grave. My Re - deem - er lives, my Re-
Bsus
B
E
A
29
deem - er lives; My Re - deem - er lives, my Re-
C♯m7
Bsus
E
A
31
1
D.C.
2
D.S.
deem - er lives. deem - er lives. My Re -
C♯m7
Bsus
C♯m7
Bsus
3
37
BRIDGE
deem - er lives. You lift my bur - den,
C♯m7
Bsus
D

41
and I rise with You; I'm danc-ing on this moun - tain - top to
A/C♯
E/B
F♯m7
see Your king - dom come. My Re -
E/G♯
Bsus
B
46
CHORUS
deem - er lives, my Re - deem - er lives; My Re -
E
A
C♯m7
Bsus
50
deem - er lives, my Re - deem - er lives. My Re -
E
A
C♯m7
Bsus

54
deem - er lives, my Re - deem - er lives; My Re -
E
A
C♯m7
Bsus
58
deem - er lives, my Re - deem - er lives. My Re -
E
A
C♯m7
Bsus
62
deem - er lives, my Re - deem - er lives; My Re -
E2
A2
C♯m7
Bsus
66
deem - er lives, my Re - deem - er lives. My Re -
E2
A2
C♯m7
Bsus

Medley Options: Who Shall Separate Us; Arise, Shine.

...Marvelous are Your works, And that my soul knows very well. Psalm 139:14 NKJ

My Savior's Love

Words and Music by
CHARLES H. GABRIEL

love me, a sin-ner, con-demned, and so un-clean.
Cal - va-ry and He suf-fer'd and died a - lone.
Am7
Dm Bbm6/Db
F/C
Bb/C
F
Bb/C
13
CHORUS
All
W.L. ad libs
O, how mar-vel - ous, how won-der - ful,
F
Am7
Dm
and my song shall ev - er be;
17
O, how mar-vel - ous,
Gm
Gm/F
Ebmaj7
C 7sus
F

how won-der - ful is my Sav - ior's love for
Am7
Dm7
Gm7
F/C
C
21
1.
2.
me.
me.
F
B♭/F
B♭m/F
F
C/D
24
CHORUS
All
W.L. ad libs
O, how mar-vel - ous, how won-der - ful, and my song shall
G
Bm7
Em7
Am
Am/G
28
ev - er be; O, how mar-vel - ous, how won-der - ful
Fmaj7
D7sus
G
Bm7
Em7

Medley options: Take A Little Time; O The Blood Of Jesus.

My soul will be satisfied as with the richest of foods; with singing lips my mouth will praise you. Psa. 63:5 NIV

My Soul Is Satisfied

Words and Music by
ED KERR

1.
back a - gain, now my soul is sat - is - fied. 2. You have
fore your throne, and my soul is sat - is -
A♭maj7 G7/B Cm7 Fm7 B♭7sus E♭
2.
14
CHORUS
fied. I was stand - ing far off when You found me;
E♭ A♭2 E♭2/G E♭/G
18
I ex - pect - ed wrath, but mer - cy flowed; This prod - i - gal re - turned be -
A♭ A♭/B♭ E♭ A♭
cause You loved me first, find - ing me, sav - ing me. 3., 4. Now my
Fm7 D♭maj7 B♭7sus Gm

22
VERSE
on - ly goal is to hon - or You, in the way I live and the
Cm Gsus/B♭ A♭ B♭ Cm7 Fm7 B♭
26
things I do; Let my life re - flect all I've found in You, How my
Fm7 B♭ Gm Cm Gm/B♭ A♭maj7 G7/B Cm7
last time to Coda
30
soul is sat - is - fied.
Fm7 B♭7sus E♭ Cm Gsus/B♭
34
A♭ B♭ Cm7 Fm7 B♭ Fm7 B♭ Gm Cm Gm/B♭

A♭maj7 G7/B Cm7 Fm7 E♭
D.S. al Coda
Coda
39
fied. Let my life re - flect all I've found in You, how my
E♭ Cm Gsus/B♭ A♭maj7 G7/B Cm7
3
soul's at peace, and my heart is full of joy; Yes, my
Fm7 B♭7sus Fm7 B♭ Gm
43
soul is sat - is - fied.
Fm7 B♭7sus E♭ Cm Gsus/B♭

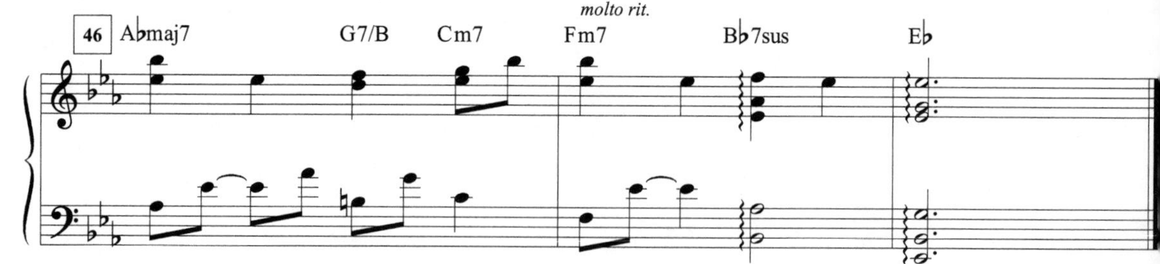

Medley options: I Was Made To Praise You.

Behold, God is my salvation; I will trust, and not be afraid. Isaiah 12:2 (KJV)

O God

Words and Music by
CRAIG SMITH

9
You bring light to pierce the dark - ness,
a crown of beau - ty in - stead of ash - es,
F/A
B♭
1.
13
You bring grace for all to see. O God,
Your garment of praise cov - ers me.
F/C
B♭/D
F/A
O God.
B♭
F/C
B♭/D

2.
All
18
CHORUS
O God, Father God; O God, Father God.
22
Bb/D
Eb
Bb
F
26
VERSE
W.L.
3. You bring streams into the desert,
F/A

cause the har - vest fields to grow;
F/C
B♭/D
30
When You breathe, life is a - bun - dant,
F/A
B♭
You cause the riv - ers of life to flow.
All
O
F/C
B♭/D
E♭
B♭
34
CHORUS
God, Fa - ther O
F
B♭
E♭
B♭
F

38
O God, Fa - ther
B♭ E♭ B♭ F B♭ E♭ B♭
God.
F B♭
42
BRIDGE 1st time instrumental
2nd time Praise Team
Bah dah bah dah, bah dah pah dah bah; Bah dah bah dah, bah dah pah dah bah;
F/A B♭
Bah dah bah dah, bah dah pah dah bah; Bah dah bah dah, bah dah pah dah bah;
F/C B♭/D

46
Worship Leader
3rd time W.L. ad libs
Give us this day our dai - ly bread,
Praise Team
Bah dah bah dah, bah dah pah dah bah; Bah dah bah dah, bah dah pah dah bah;
F/A
Bb
O God our pro - vi - der; O
1, 2.
Bah dah bah dah, bah dah pah dah bah; Bah dah bah O
F/C
Bb
Eb Bb
3.
51 CHORUS
1st time instrumental
2nd time All
der; O God,
Fa - ther
Bah dah bah O God,
Optional: Percussion only for 8 bars
Optional: 2nd time band plays
Bb
Eb Bb
F
Bb
Eb Bb

55
God;
O
God,
F
B♭
E♭
B♭
F
1, 2.
Sing both times
Fa - ther
God.
O
B♭
E♭
B♭
F
B♭
E♭
B♭
Optional Band re-enters
3.
God,
God.
F
F
B♭
62
F/A
B♭
F/C

Medley options: Above All Else; With All Faith Believe.

Who shall separate us from the love of Christ?.... Romans 8:35 (NIV)

O The Passion

Words and Music by
DAVID BARONI
and GARY SADLER

15
Who are we that He would love us? Who, but He would
D/F♯ G(add9) D/A Bm Em7 D/F♯
19
give His life?
G(add9) Asus A
O the pas-sion,
D Em7 D/F♯
22
O the won-der of the fie-ry love of Christ.
G(add9) Asus G/B D/A Asus D
26
G/D D G/D
29 VERSE 2
2. O the wis-dom,
D

33
37
41
O the won - der of the pow - er of the cross;
G/D
G(add9)
D
Asus
A
Love so rare no words could tell it, Life Him-self has
D
G(add9)
Asus
G(add9)/B
D/A
died for us. Who are we that He would save us?
Asus
D
D/F♯
G(add9)
Asus
D/A
Cru - ci-fied to give us life;
Em7
D/F♯
G
Asus
A

O the wis - dom, O the won - der of the pow - er
D Em7 D/F♯ G(add9) Asus G/B Asus
45
of the cross.
A D D/A G/D Em7
50 VERSE 3
3. O the pas - sion, O the won - der
D D/A G/D Em7 D G/D
54
of the fie - ry love of Christ; Death de-feat - ed by His ris - ing,
G(add9) Bm7 Asus A D G(add9) D

58
darkness conquered by His light. We will sing His
G(add9) D Asus D D/F♯ G(add9)
praise forever, worthy is the Lamb of Life;
Asus Bm7 Em7 D/F♯ G(add9)
62
O the passion, O the wonder
Asus A D Em7 D/F♯ G(add9) A D/A
67
of the fiery love of Christ. Who are we that
G(add9)/B Asus D D/F♯ G

Medley Options: My Jesus, I Love Thee; Lead Me to the Cross.

For You are great, and do wondrous things; You alone are God. Psalm 86:10 (NKJ)

Only You

Words and Music by
CRAIG SMITH

9
hands to a tree; You left a path - way for
A2
E
C♯m7
Bsus
Your friends to fol - low, marked by the blood spilled for the
A2
E
C♯m7
Bsus
13
whole world to see;
A2
E
C♯m7
Bsus
A2
E
C♯m7
Bsus
A2
E

17
VERSE
W.L.
2. There are some— who have in-jured and— harmed— us,
W.L.
3. We come be-fore— You bro-ken and— hum-ble,
C♯m7
Bsus
A2
E
will-ful in-ten-tions to— hurt and of-fend;— O, but
our hearts are— heav-y from the suff-'ring we've caused;— With
C♯m7
Bsus
A2
E
21
Your way is— love,— and— Your way is— right-eous, so
shame we con-fess,— re-pent, we have— stum-bled,—
C♯m7
Bsus
A2
E

we ex - tend mer - cy and re - fuse to con - demn.
P.T. Male soloist, top note
Fa - ther, for - give us and re - deem what was lost.
C♯m7
Bsus
A2
E
25
CHORUS
W.L.
On - ly You can give us our free - dom; On - ly You can
Praise Team
On - ly You, Oo; On - ly You,
A
E
B
C♯m7
A
E
29
par - don from sin; On - ly You re - turn the joy of sal - va - tion,
Oo; On - ly You, Oo;
B
E
A
E
B
C♯m7

last time to Coda
31
1.
we need the grace which comes on - ly from You;
we need the grace on - ly from You;
A
E
B
C♯m7
We need the grace which comes on-ly from You.
35
we need the grace on-ly from You.
A
E
B
C♯m7
Bsus
A2
E
C♯m7
Bsus

2.
D.S. al Coda
on - ly from You.
on - ly from You.
A2
E
B
E
Coda
41
W.L. and Praise Team Ladies
on - ly from You.
We need the grace which comes
on - ly from You.
we need the grace
B
E
A
E
W.L. only
on-ly from You.
We need the grace which comes on-ly from
on-ly from You.
we need the grace
B
E
A
E
B

Medley options: I Need You More; Nothing But The Blood.

1247

Who is like the LORD our God, the One who sits enthroned on high? Psa. 113:5 NIV

Praise Adonai

Words and Music by
PAUL BALOCHE

2nd time - Worship Leader and Ladies

ev - 'ry o - cean roars to the Lord of hosts.

F C G

13 **CHORUS**

All

Praise A - do - nai, from the ris - ing of the sun 'til the

F Am G

end of ev - 'ry day;

17 *1st time - Melody and Tenor only*

2nd time - 3 part

Praise A - do - nai, all the

Dm7 F G F Am

na - tions of the earth, all the an - gels and the saints sing praise.

1.

G Dm7 F G B♭2

2.
praise.
B♭2
B♭2
25
B♭
Am
C
G
29
B♭
Am
33
CHORUS
Praise
A - do -
F
G
F

nai, from the ris-ing of the sun 'til the end of ev - 'ry day;
Am
G
Dm7
F G
37
Praise A-do - nai, all the na-tions of the earth, all the
F
Am
G
41
CHORUS
an-gels and the saints sing, Praise A-do - nai, from the
Dm7
F G
F
Am
45
ris-ing of the sun 'til the end of ev - 'ry day; Praise A-do -
G
Dm7
F G
F

Medley options: Lift Him Up; I Will Celebrate (BALOCHE).

...They raised their voices in praise to the LORD and sang: "He is good; his love endures forever..." 2 Chronicles 5:13 NIV

Praise To The Lord

Words and Music by
BOB FITTS

14
2nd time - Men add lower note
When I am bro - ken, Lord,
You are my
F
18
strength, You're my strength; You're my love, You're my life,
C
F2/A
B♭
Gm7
2nd time - All
2nd time - W. L. and Men
You're my joy, my song in the night; How I
F2/A
B♭2
F/A

22
2nd time - All
mar - vel at Your mer - cy and I sing,
Gm7
E♭maj7
B♭/D
Csus
C
26
CHORUS
All
Praise,
praise to the
B♭/C C B♭/C C
F
Lord;
30
Praise,
B♭
F
praise to the Lord;
For
B♭

34
He is good and mer-ci-ful, His love is great, He's so
Gm7(add4)
Csus
C
C/D
Gm7(add4)
last time to Coda
38
won-der-ful, my Lord.
Csus
C
F
1.
Worship Leader
2.
D.S. al Coda
In these
Dm
C
B♭
Dm
C
B♭

Medley options: He Will Come And Save You; Pure In Heart.

Be my rock of refuge, to which I can always go... Psa. 71:3 NIV

Rock Of Refuge

Words and Music by
GARY SADLER

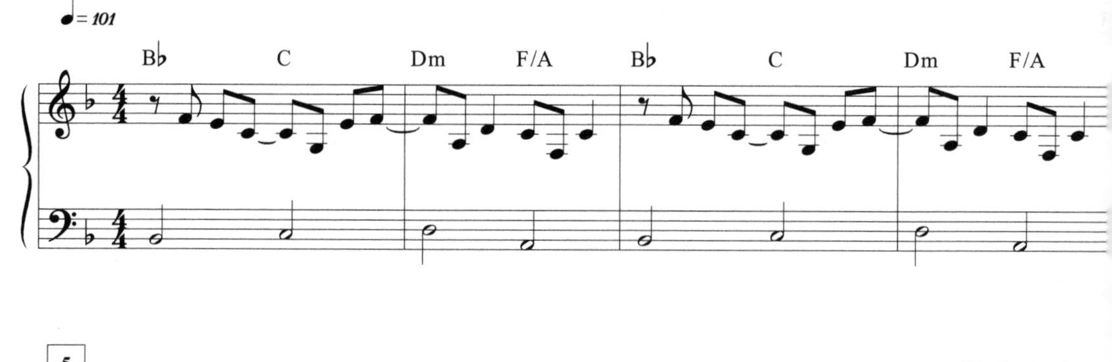

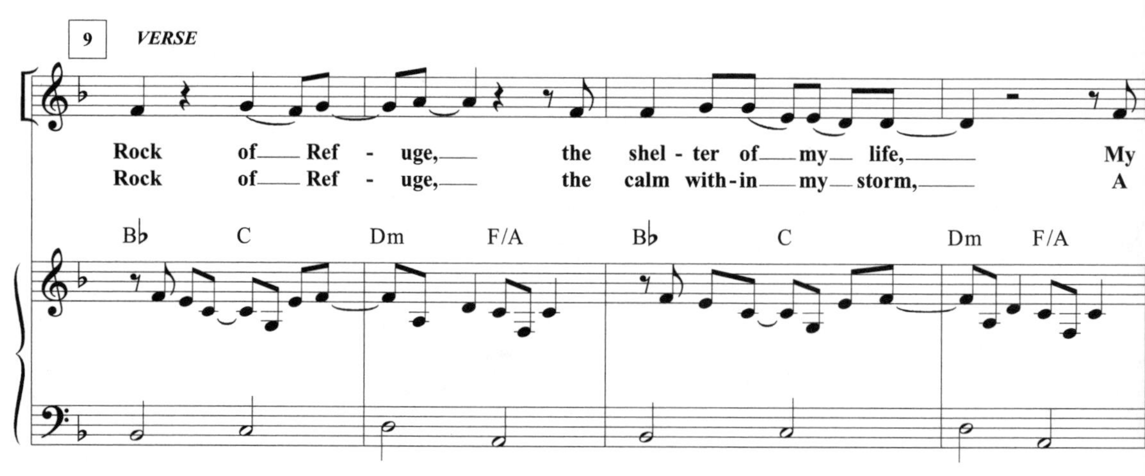

13
mer - ci - ful com - pan - ion, my com - fort in the night;
se - cret place of safe - ty, my bar - ri - er from harm;
B♭ C Dm F/A B♭ C
17
2nd time - All
Though my heart falls hard, still Your
When my eyes are tears, through my
Dm F/A B♭ C Dm F/A
21
love stands guard,
worst of fears,
O Lord, You are
B♭ C Gm7 B♭ C
my Rock of Ref - uge. And I
Dm F/A B♭ C F

25
CHORUS
All
run to You, and You hold me close,
C
F
Dm
29
You hide me under Your
B♭
F
Gm7(add4)
32
shad - ow. Yes, I run to You,
C 7sus
F
E♭maj9
it's so good to know, O Lord,
Dm
B♭

Medley options: My Eyes Are Fixed On You; I Can Do All Things (SMITH).

Oh, clap your hands, all you peoples! Shout to God with the voice of triumph! Psalm 47:1 (NKJ)

Shout

Words and Music by
MARTHA MUNIZZI

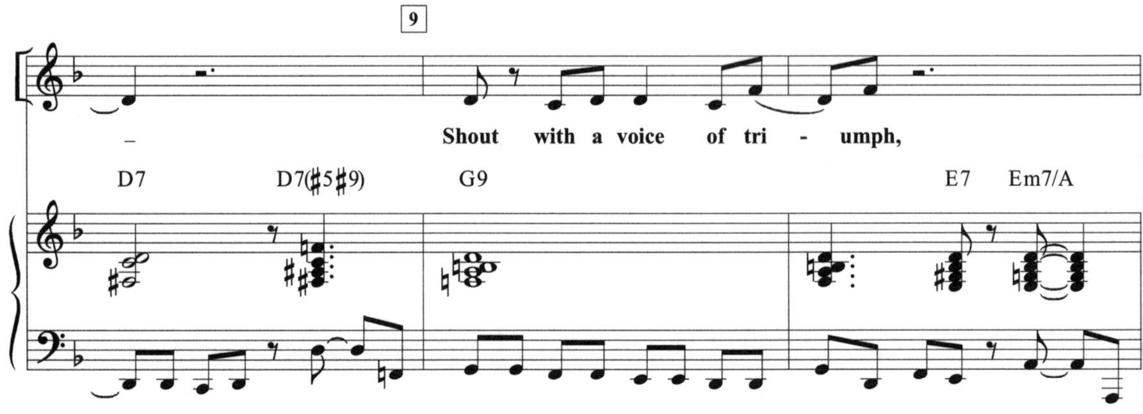

13
Shout with a voice of praise;
Shout un - to God for the
D9sus
D7
A7
last time to Coda
vic - to - ry;
Hey hey,
Give the Lord a shout of praise;
A♭7
G7
N.C.
1.
2, 3.
19
VERSE
Tri - um - phant in bat - tle,
A7(♯5)
A7(♯5)
Dm
We are vic - to - rious;
God is most high
ov - er
all the earth;
E7(♭9)
A7

23
Melody - bottom note
Je - sus has con-quered, Sa-tan's de-feat-ed; The en - e - my is un-der my feet,
Dm
Em7 Dm/F G7 A7sus
So I will
4, 5.
A7(♯5)
28 BRIDGE
Worship Leader ad libs
Dm
Gsus/D Dm F2 G2 A2
32
Praise Team
Shout for the vic-to-ry, Shout if you've been set free; Shout!
Dm
Gsus/D Dm

36
Shout for the vic-to-ry,
Shout if you've been set free;
Shout!
F2
G2
A2
Dm
1.
40
Shout for the vic - to - ry,
Gsus/D
Dm
F2
G2
A2
Dm
D.S.
Shout if you've been set free;
Shout!
Gsus/D
Dm
A7(♯5)
2.
46
Shout for the vic - to - ry,
F2
G2
A2
Dm

D.S. al Coda
Shout if you've been set free; Shout!
Dm
Coda
50
CHORUS
Give the Lord a shout
Shout with a voice of tri - umph,
N.C.
D9sus
D7
54
Shout with a voice of praise;
Shout with a voice of tri -
D9sus
D7
D7(♯5♯9)
G9
umph,
Shout with a voice of praise;
E7
Em7/A
D9sus
D7

Medley options: Not By Power (CHISUM/SADLER); Come Into This House.

...Speak, Lord, for your servant is listening... 1 Samuel 3:9 (NIV)

Speak Lord

Words and Music by
BISHOP CLARENCE MCCLENDON

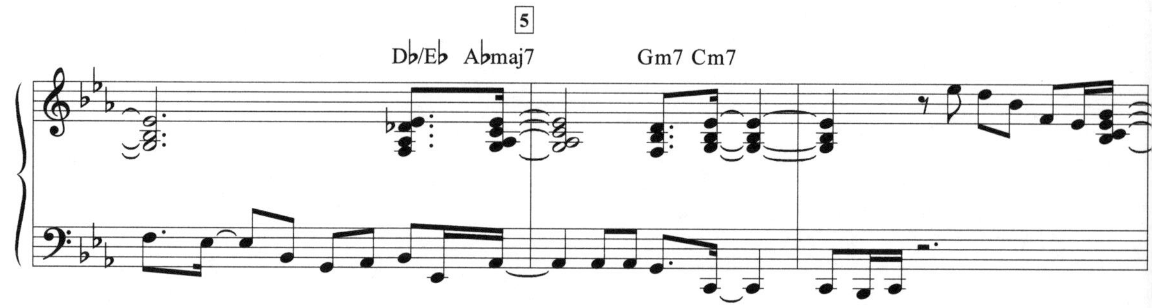

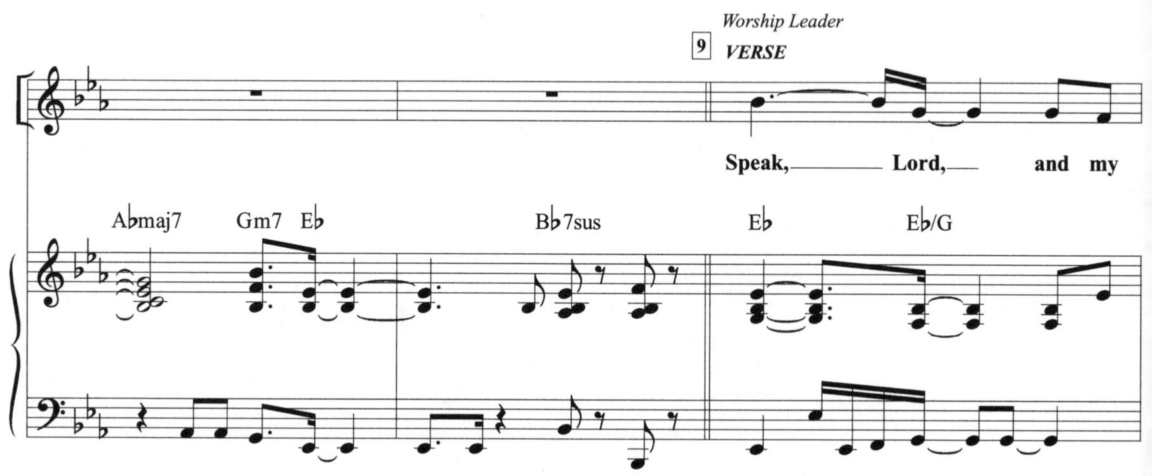

heart will o-bey The words that You speak in-to my heart to-day; My
Ab Eb/G Eb Ab Cm7 F/A Bb7sus Eb

13
heart is o - pen wide, and I know that when You speak You'll pro - vide for my
Ab Cm7 Gm7(b5) C7(b9)

eve - ry need; I know You'll meet my eve - ry
Fm7 Eb/G Bb/C N.C. Fm7 Eb/G Fm/Ab Eb/Bb Bb

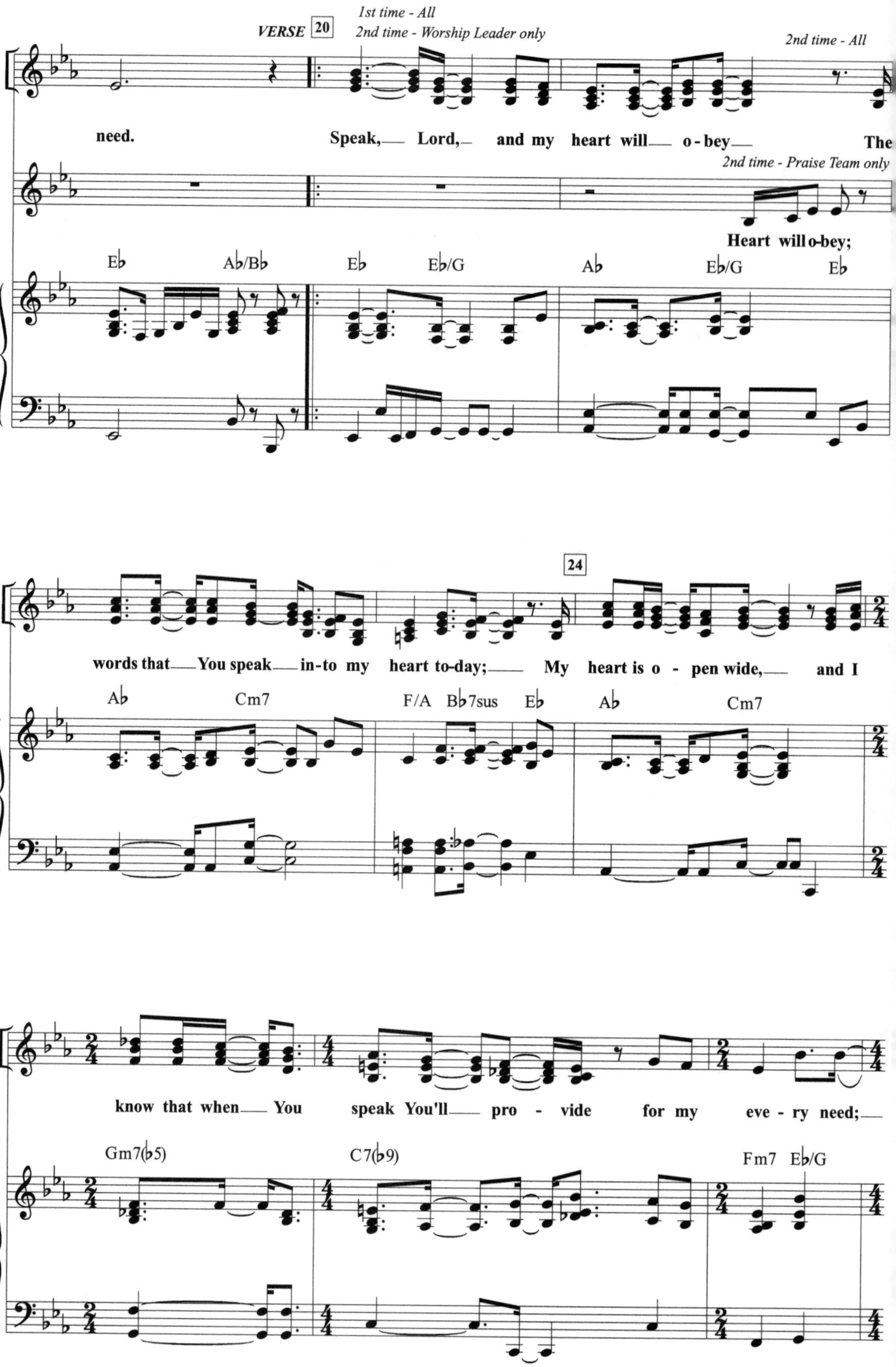
VERSE
20
1st time - All
2nd time - Worship Leader only
2nd time - All
need. Speak, Lord, and my heart will o - bey The
2nd time - Praise Team only
Heart will o-bey;
E♭ A♭/B♭ E♭ E♭/G A♭ E♭/G E♭
24
words that You speak in-to my heart to-day; My heart is o - pen wide, and I
A♭ Cm7 F/A B♭7sus E♭ A♭ Cm7
know that when You speak You'll pro - vide for my eve - ry need;
Gm7(♭5) C7(♭9) Fm7 E♭/G

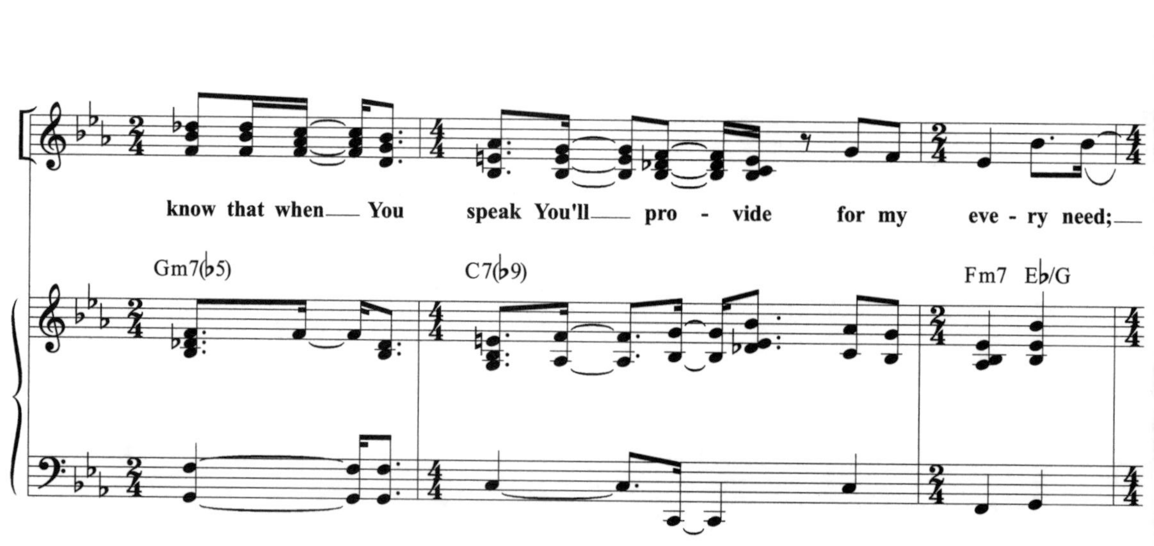

28
I know You'll meet my eve - ry need.
Bb/C
N.C.
Fm7
Eb/G
Fm/Ab
Eb/Bb
Bb
Ebsus
Eb
31
CHORUS
Choir
Hal-le-lu - jah,
Hal - le - lu-jah,
Hal - le-lu - jah,
Praise Team - Add 2nd time
Hal-le - lu-jah,
Hal - le - lu-jah,
Ab
Eb/G Cm7
Fm7 Ab/Bb
Eb
Eb/G
Ab
Eb/G Cm7
35
Hal - le - lu-jah;
Hal-le-lu - jah,
Hal - le - lu-jah,
Hal-le - lu,
Fm7 Ab/Bb
Eb
Eb/G
Ab
Eb/G Cm7
Fm7 Ab/Bb
Eb
Eb/G

37
1.
2, 3.
Hal-le-lu - jah, Hal - le - lu-jah; Hal - le - lu-jah;
Hal - le - lu,
A♭ E♭/G Cm7 Fm7 A♭/B♭ E♭ Fm7 A♭/B♭ E♭
40
Thank You, Je - sus, Thank You, Je - sus;
Thank You, Je - sus, Je - sus;
A♭ E♭/G Cm7 Fm7 A♭/B♭ E♭ E♭/G
Thank You, Je - sus, Thank You, Je - sus;
Thank You, Je - sus, Je - sus;
A♭ E♭/G Cm7 Fm7 A♭/B♭ E♭ E♭/G

44
Thank You, Je - sus,
Thank You, Je - sus;
Thank You, Je - sus, Je - sus;
Ab Eb/G Cm7 Fm7 Ab/Bb Eb Eb/G
Thank You, Je - sus,
Thank You, Je - sus.
Thank You, Je - sus, Je - sus;
Ab Eb/G Cm7 Fm7 Ab/Bb Eb
48
Hal - le - lu - jah, Hal - le - lu-jah,
Hal - le - lu - jah,
Hal - le - lu-jah,
Hal - le - lu - jah,
Ab Eb/G Cm7 Fm7 Ab/Bb Eb Eb/G Ab Eb/G Cm7

52
Hal - le - lu - jah;
Hal - le - lu - jah,
Hal - le - lu,
Fm7 Ab/Bb Eb Eb/G Ab Eb/G Cm7
Hal - le - lu - jah,
2nd time only - Women
Bop bop bah dee;
Hal - le - lu - jah,
Hal - le - lu,
Fm7 Ab/Bb Eb Eb/G Ab Eb/G Cm7
last time to Coda
56
Worship Leader
VERSE
Hal - le - lu - jah;
Speak, Lord, and my
Praise Team
Speak to my heart, Lord,
Fm7 Ab/Bb Eb Eb2 Eb2/G

heart will — o - bey The words that — You speak in - to my
Heart — will o - bey, words that — You speak
A♭ E♭/G E♭ A♭ Cm7
60
heart to - day; — My heart is o - pen wide, — and I
You know — my heart o - o - pen wide, — and I
F/A B♭7sus E♭ A♭ Cm7
All
W.L.
know that when — You speak You'll — pro - vide for my
Gm7(♭5) C7(♭9)

Medley options: No Eye Has Seen (CHISUM/SADLER); Why So Downcast.

And suddenly there came a sound from heaven, as of a rushing mighty wind, and it filled the whole house where they were sitting. Acts 2:2 (NKJ)

Suddenly

Words and Music by
ALVIN SLAUGHTER and ROGER RYAN

Pray - ing for God's pow - er from on high;
When it seems you don't have strength to car - ry
G
G/B
C2
Em7
11
They were wait - ing for a prom - ise made
on; There is glo - ry in God's pre - sence, there is
F2
D/F♯
G
Am7(add4)
G/B
not so long a - go;
Je - sus
heal - ing in His Word;
He's our
C
G
G/B

15
said that He would set their souls on fire;
an - chor and our peace in ev - ery storm;
C2
Em9
F
E/G♯
Sud-den-ly the sound of the wind came rush-ing in, and their
So, my friend, call on the Lord and trust His Word Age to
Am
Am/G
D/F♯
D
19
souls were set a - flame; To
age He's still the same, for He's a
G
G/B
C2

them He gave the pow - er, when they
God that hears us, and a God that loves us; There's
Am7
G/B
molto rit.
called up - on His name.
pow - er in His name.
C2
D 7sus
24
CHORUS
a tempo
Sud-den-ly, I can feel His might - y pow - er;
G2
G/B
C
Em7

Sud-den-ly, I can feel the change within, and I know
Am7
Am7/G
F♯m7(♭5)
Am/B
B7(♭9)
28
Second time to Coda
that I will nev - er, ev-er be the same a - gain;
Em
Em/D
Am7
Dsus
D/F♯
You can find what You need at the al - tar;
G2
G/B
C
Em7
32
Leave be-hind ev-ery weight that press - es in, For the Spir -
Am7
Am7/G
F♯m7(♭5)
Am/B
B7(♭9)

it of the Lord is still mov - ing, Sud - den -
Em
Em/D
A/C♯
Cm/D
36
ly.
G
E♭maj7
F
Coda
39
be the same a - gain; You can find what You
Am7
E♭/F
F/A
B♭2
B♭/D
need at the al - tar; Leave be - hind ev - ery
E♭
Gm7
Cm7
Cm7/B♭

43
weight that press - es in, For the Spir - it of the Lord is still
Am7(♭5)
Cm/D D7(♭9)
Gm
Gm/F
mov - ing, For the Spir - it of the Lord is still
C/E
F/E♭
Dm7(♭5)
Fm/A♭
47
mov - ing, Yes, the Spir - it of the Lord is still
G
G7(♯5♭9)
Cm7
B♭/D
E♭
C2/E
molto rit.
mov - ing sud - den - ly.
E♭/F
E♭m/F

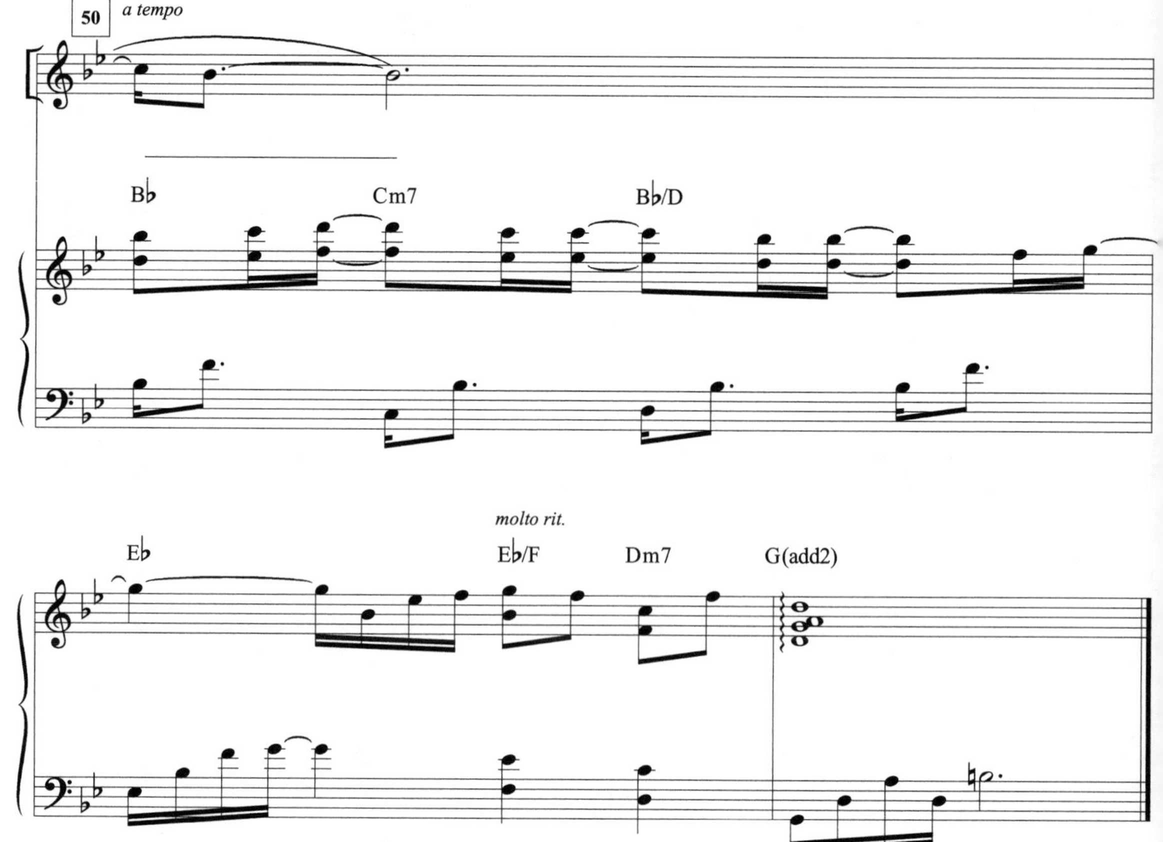

Medley option: There Is A Fountain Filled With Blood.

Therefore God also has highly exalted Him and given Him the name which is above every name.... Philippians 2:9 (NKJV)

The Name Of Jesus

Words and Music by
CHRIS WRIGHT

CHORUS
1st time - Soloist only
2nd and 3rd times - All
13
Jesus. And we cry, "Holy, holy, holy, is the
Holy, holy, holy,
F C Am C/G
Lord our God." And we sing, "Worthy is the Lamb, Who was slain."
Ooo; Worthy is the Lamb, Who was slain.
F C Am
17
And we shout, "Glory, glory, glory, to the
Glory, glory, glory,
G Am C/G

last time to Coda
King of kings."
Ooo;
The name above all names,
The name above all names,
F
C
G
Am
F
21
the name of Je - sus.
Je - sus.
1
Gsus
G
C
C/E
F
Am
G
VERSE 2
Soloist
25
2. Now, we sing the prais - es of the
C
C/E
F
C
C/E

One that we love;
Je - sus,
F
C
G
29
We sing the prais - es of the
Je - sus.
F
C
C/E
One that we love.
And we cry,
Je - sus,
Je - sus.
F
C
G
F
C

E7
F
E7
F
F/G
C
C/E
F
Am
G
VERSE 3
Soloist
3. And there's might - y pow - er when we call on His name;
Soloist 2
Call on
C
C/E
F
C
O, my Je - sus.
Je - sus, we call on Je - sus.
G
F
C

43
Pow - er to heal, for - give, and pow - er to save;
We call on
C/E
F
C
Je - sus!
Je - sus,
His name is Je - sus!
G
F
C
Coda
47
the name a - bove all names.
And we cry,
The name a - bove all names.
G
Am
F
Gsus
G

"Ho - ly, ho - ly, ho - ly, is the Lord our God."
Ho - ly, ho - ly, ho - ly,
Ooo.
Am
C/G
F
C
The name a - bove all names, the name of Je - sus.
The name a - bove all names, Je - sus.
G
Am
F
Am
G
The name of Je - sus.
C
C/E
F
Am
G

Medley Options: Resound in Praise; I Will Sing (WILLARD/ROGERS).

....Do not sorrow, for the joy of the Lord is your strength. Nehemiah 8:10 (NKJV)

Trading My Sorrows

Words and Music by
DARRELL EVANS

last time to Coda
down for the joy of the Lord.
down for the joy of the Lord.
Em D G C Em D
13
Yes, Lord, yes, Lord, yes, yes, Lord; Yes, Lord, yes, Lord,
G C Em D G C
17
yes, yes, Lord; Yes, Lord, yes, Lord, yes, yes, Lord, A -
Em D/F♯ G C Em D
1
21
VERSE
Solo
men. I'm pressed but not crushed, per-se -
G C Em D G C

cu-ted, not a-ban-doned, struck down, but not de - stroyed; I'm
Em D G C Em D/F♯
25
blessed be - yond the curse, for His prom - ise will en - dure, that His
G C Em D
29
joy's gon-na be my strength. Though the sor - row may
G C Em D
last for the night, His joy comes with the morn - ing.
Dsus D F C

34
2
Yes, Lord, yes, Lord, yes, yes, Lord;
Em D G C Em D
38
Yes, Lord, yes, Lord, yes, yes, Lord,
Yes, Lord, yes, Lord,
G C Em D/F♯ G C
yes, yes, Lord, A - men.
Em D G C Em D
42
G C Em D G C Em D/F♯

G C Em D G C Em D
Solo
Though the sor - row may last for the night, His
Dsus D
joy comes with the morn - ing.
F C
Coda
54
All
La, la, la, la, la, la, la, la, la, la, la, la,
Em D G C Em D

59
la, la, la, la, la, la, la, la, la, la; La, la, la, la, la, la, la,
G C Em D/F♯ G C
la, la, la, la, A - men. La,
Em D G C Em D
63
la, la, la, la, la, la, la, la, la, la, la, la, la, la, la, la, la, la,
G C Em D G C
67
la, la, la, la; La, la, la, la, la, la, la, la, la, la, la, A -
Em D/F♯ G C Em D

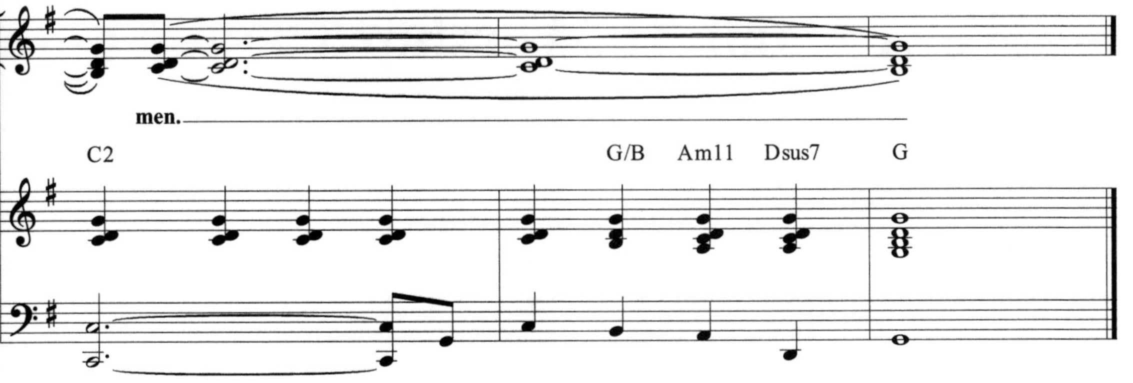

Medley Options: Whom Shall I Fear; The Happy Song.

1255

Ascribe to the Lord the glory due his name; worship the Lord in the splendor of his holiness. Psalm 29:2 (NIV)

We've Come To Worship The Lord

Words and Music by
DAVID HORTON

Medley options: Lord, I Thirst For You; Lord, I Come.

Therefore I will praise You among the nations, O LORD; I will sing praises to Your name. Psa. 18:49 NIV

We Offer Praises

Words and Music by
RON KENOLY

All
1
2
praised.
We of - fer
praised.
Cmaj7
B♭11 E♭maj7 Dm7
G11
Cmaj7
Fm7 B♭7 Cmaj7
W.L.
16
You are ho - ly and wor - thy to be
glo - ri - ous with end - less love, You are
Dm7
B♭maj7
20
wor - shipped and a - dored,
right - eous - ness and truth,
yes - ter - day, to -
Mer - cy, peace - filled
Gm7
C11
Fmaj7
Dm7
Cmaj7/E
2nd time to Coda
day, and for - ev - er - more.
joy and love a - bounds in
Fmaj7
F♯dim7
B7sus4(♭9) B7(♭9)
Em
A13(♯11) Dm7

All
25
We of - fer prais - es to You, Al-might - y
G11
Cmaj7
Dm7
29
God, Now and for - ev - er, You're
Cmaj7/E
Fmaj7
G11
F/G
Em7
Am7
ho - ly and wor-thy to be praised.
Dm7
G11
Cmaj7
B♭11
E♭maj7
Dm7
G11
33
Cmaj7
Dm7
Cmaj7/E
Fmaj7
G11
Dm/G

37
D.S. al Coda
W.L.
You are
Em7 Am7 Dm7 G11 Cmaj7 Fm7 B♭7 Cmaj7
Coda
All
43
You. We of-fer prais - es to You, Al-might-y
Em A11 F♯m7 Em7 A11 Dmaj7 Em7
47
God, Now and for - ev - er, You're
Dmaj7/F♯ Gmaj7 A11 G/A F♯m7 Bm7
1
ho - ly and wor-thy to be praised. We of - fer
Em7 A11 Dmaj7 C11 Fmaj7 Em7 A11

Medley Option: Ancient Of Days

Let all those who seek You rejoice and be glad in You... Psalm 70:4 NKJ

We Seek Your Face

Words and Music by
MARK CONDON

10
ness; Lord of mer - cy and a-maz-ing grace, we bow
A A Bm/A A Bm/A
1. 2. All - Men sing melody
down and seek Your face. Heav-en-ly face. Heav-en-ly
A Bm/E A A
15 CHORUS
Fa-ther, God of right-eous - ness, we are hun - gry for Your ho-li -
A Bm/A A Bm/A A Bm/E
19
ness; Lord of mer - cy and a-maz-ing grace, we bow
A A Bm/A A Bm/A

down
and seek Your
face;
A
Bm/E
A
C♯m7(♯5)
23
VERSE
Ladies
1. Lord, we love You and we're here to give You praise;
Ladies
2. There's no oth - er that could ev - er take Your place;
D
A2/C♯
Bm7
E/G♯
A
Lord, we wor - ship You for the rest of our
You're the Mas - ter of it all, You de - serve the high - est
D
A2/C♯
Bm7
C♯m7
D

1.
All - Men sing melody
2.
All - Men sing melody
days. Heav-en - ly
praise.
Heav - en - ly
Bm7/E
N.C.
Bm7/E
29
CHORUS
Fa-ther, God of right-eous - ness, we are hun - gry for Your ho-li -
B♭
Cm/B♭
B♭
Cm/B♭
B♭
Cm/F
ness; Lord of
33
mer - cy and a-maz-ing grace, we bow
B♭
B♭
Cm/B♭
B♭
Cm/B♭
down and seek Your face; Heav-en - ly
B♭
Cm/F
B♭
E/F♯

37
CHORUS
Fa-ther, God of right-eous - ness, we are hun - gry for Your ho-li -
B
C♯m/B
B
C♯m/B
B
C♯m/F♯
41
ness; Lord of mer - cy and a-maz-ing grace, we bow
B
B
C♯m/B
B
C♯m/B
45
down and seek Your face; We bow down and seek Your
B
C♯m/F♯
B
B/F♯
C♯m/F♯
Gradual decrescendo
face; We bow down and seek Your face; We bow
B
C♯m/B
B/F♯
C♯m/F♯
B
C♯m/B

49
Subito forte
down and seek Your face.
Heav-en - ly
B/F♯
F♯7sus
B
F/G
52 CHORUS
Fa-ther, God of right-eous - ness, we are hun - gry for Your ho-li -
C
Dm/C
C
Dm/C
C
Dm/G
56
ness; Lord of mer - cy and a-maz-ing grace, we bow
C
C
Dm/C
C
Dm/C
down and seek Your face; We bow
C
Dm/G
C

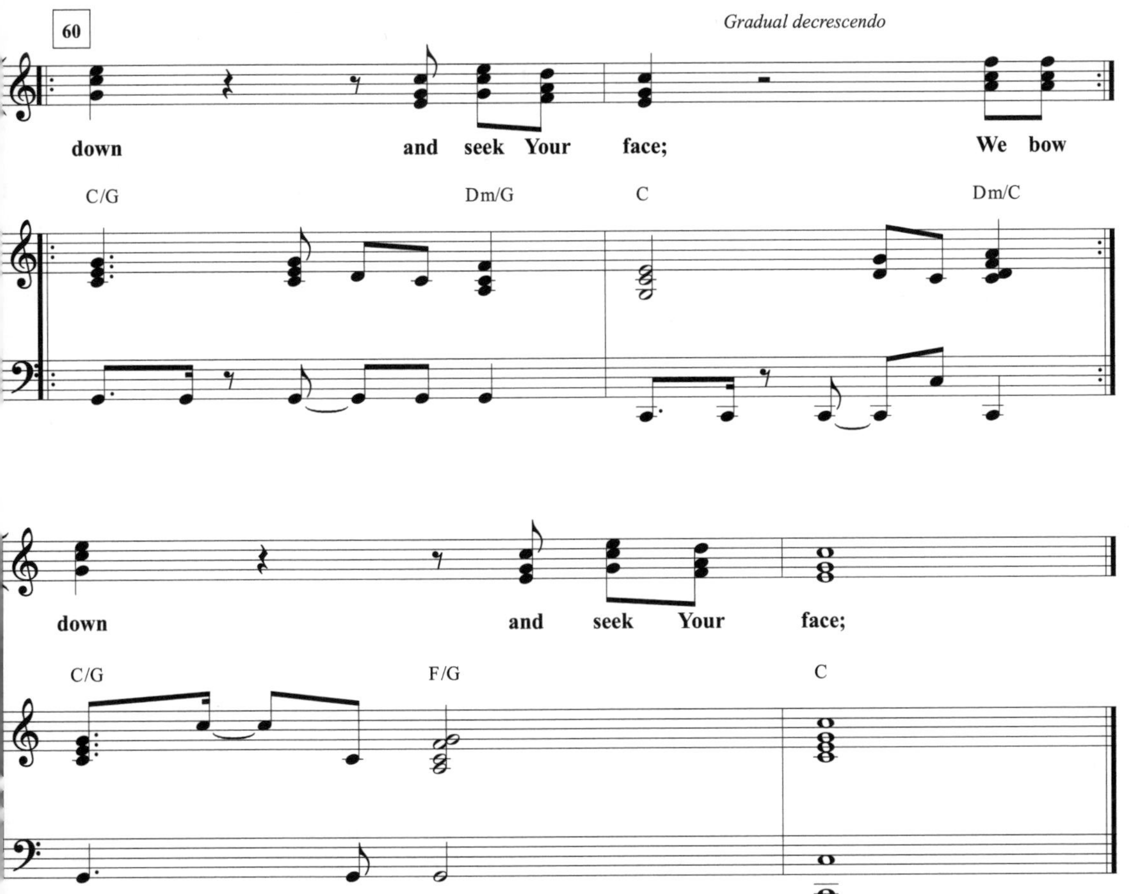

Medley options: Righteousness, Peace, Joy.

Be thou exalted, Lord, in thine own strength: so will we sing and praise thy power. Psalm 21:13 (KJV)

We Sing

Words and Music by
CRAIG SMITH

1.
An - cient of Days, on the wings of the wind You ride;
We sing,
mountains sing, the re - deemed of the Lord lift their
D5
Em7
D5
13
Oo,
and we dance.
G5
D5
Em7
17
VERSE
You cause the bar - ren des - ert to bloom, turn the
D5
G5
D5

21
sea in - to dry land;
Your voice has raised the
Em7
D5
G5
dead from the tomb, e - vil flees when You com - mand.
And we sing,
D5
Em7
D5
25
CHORUS
we sing,
we clap,
and cry out;
We sing,
we dance,
we clap,
G5
D5
Em7
29
We kneel,
we bow,
we shout,
cry out;
We kneel,
we bow,
C
G5
D5

32
All
we shout,
we de - clare the King - dom of our
Em7
C
G/B
Am7
God.
God.
we de - clare the King - dom of our
G5
D5
Em7
38
D5
G5
D5
2.
hands.
And we sing
Em7
D/F♯
D
C
D5

43
CHORUS - W.L. only
we dance,
we clap,
and cry out;
Praise Team
We sing,
we dance,
we clap,
G5
D5
Em7
47
We kneel,
we bow,
we shout,
cry out;
We kneel,
we bow,
C
G5
D5
1.
we praise.
We sing
2.
we shout,
we praise.
we shout,
Em7
C
Em7
All
54
we de - clare the King - dom of our God.
C
G/B
Am7
G5

G5
58
A5
E
F♯m7
W.L.
Oh, we sing,
62
CHORUS
W.L. ad libs on repeats
we dance,
we clap,
Praise Team
We sing,
we dance,
D5
A5
E5
and cry out;
We kneel,
66
we bow,
we clap,
cry out;
We kneel,
F♯m7
D
A5

Medley options: I Could Sing Of Your Love Forever.

...Salvation to our God which sitteth upon the throne, and unto the Lamb. Revelation 7:10 (KJV)

Who Can Satisfy

Words and Music by
DENNIS JERNIGAN

9
Who could ev - er be more faith-ful and true? I will trust in You,
Bbm7(add4) Db/Eb Abmaj7 Db9 Cm7 Gm7
14
CHORUS
All
Bottom note melody
I will trust in You, my God. There is a foun - tain
Cm7 Gm7 Fm7sus Ab/Bb Eb Bb/D
Who is a King, Vic-tor - ious War - rior, and Lord of ev-ery-thing;
Cm7 Bb Ab Eb/G Fm7 Bb7sus Bb
18
20
My Rock, my Shel - ter, my ver-y own, Bless-ed Re-deem - er, Who
Eb Bb/D Cm7 Bb Ab Eb/G

23
CHORUS
reigns up - on the throne.
There is a foun - tain
Fm7 E♭/G A♭ A♭/B♭
A♭/E♭
E♭
E
B/D♯
Who is a King,
Vic-tor-ious War - rior, and Lord of ev-ery-thing;
C♯m7
B
A
E/G♯
F♯m7
B 7sus B
27
My Rock, my Shel - ter, my ver-y own,
Bless-ed Re-deem - er, Who
E
B/D♯
C♯m7
B
A
E/G♯
32
VERSE
Worship Leader
reigns up - on the throne.
Who could ev - er be more
F♯m7 E/G♯ A A/B
A/E
E
E
E/G♯

35
3
faith-ful and true?
I will trust in You,
I will trust in You,
A2
D9
E/B
A/B
E/B
A/B
Worship Leader ad libs
38
CHORUS
Praise Team
I will trust in You,
my God.
There is a foun - tain
E/B
A/B
Esus
E
C7
F
A7(♯5)
Who is a King,
Vic-tor - ious War - rior,
and
Lord of ev-ery-thing;
Dm
C
B♭
F/A
Gm7
C7sus C
42
My Rock, my Shel - ter,
my ver - y own,
F
A7(♯5)
Dm
C

Medley options: Bless His Holy Name; I Bow My Knee.

There is a friend who sticks closer than a brother. Proverbs 18:24 NIV

Who's There? God's There

Words and Music by
TONY KENOLY and LOUIS SMITH

10
real, the si - lent tears you
Gm9
G7(♭5)/D♭
Cm9
cry can nev - er go un - heard,
Gm9
Cm9
Gm9
14
for God is stand - ing by
Cm9
Gm9
18
CHORUS
be-fore you say a word. Who's there?
Cm9
F11
E♭/G F/A
B♭

God's there,
Al - ways
Cm7/B♭
B♭maj7
Dm7
Gm7
22
right by your side.
Who's there?
Cm7
F11
B♭
God's there.
Cm7
F
F♯dim7
Al - ways
1
stand - ing close by.
26
VERSE
Your life may seem
Gm7
Dm7
Gm7
Cm7
B♭/D
E♭
F11
G11
Cm9

hard, when ev' - ry - thing goes
Gm9
Cm9
30
wrong, see, fear can grip your soul
Gm9
Cm9
Gm9
and your doubts can be so strong.
Cm9
Gm9
G7(♭5)/D♭
34
Re - mem - ber Je - sus knows the heart - ache that you
Cm9
Gm9
Cm9

38
feel, and He wants to hold you,
Gm9 Cm9 Gm9
un - til you heal.
2
stand - ing close by.
Cm9 F11 E♭/G F/A Cm7 B♭/D E♭ F11 G7(♭5)/D♭
43
BRIDGE
He's right there with you, stand - ing next to you, He's right there by your
Cm7 Dm7 Gm7 Cm7
47
side; So don't be a - fraid 'cause He won't go a - way,
Dm7 Gm7 G7(♭5)/D♭ Cm7 Dm7 Gm7

God's right there stand - ing by.
E♭maj7
Dm7
F/G
G
52
CHORUS
Who's there? God's there.
Cmaj7
Dm7/C
Al - ways right by your side.
Cmaj7
Em7
Am7
Dm7
G11
56
Who's there? God's there.
Cmaj7
Am7
Dm7
G11
G♯dim7

Medley Options: Center Of My Joy; I Still Have Joy

....You are the one I praise. Jeremiah 17:14 (NIV)

Wonderful, Merciful, Savior

Words and Music by
DAWN RODGERS
and ERIC WYSE

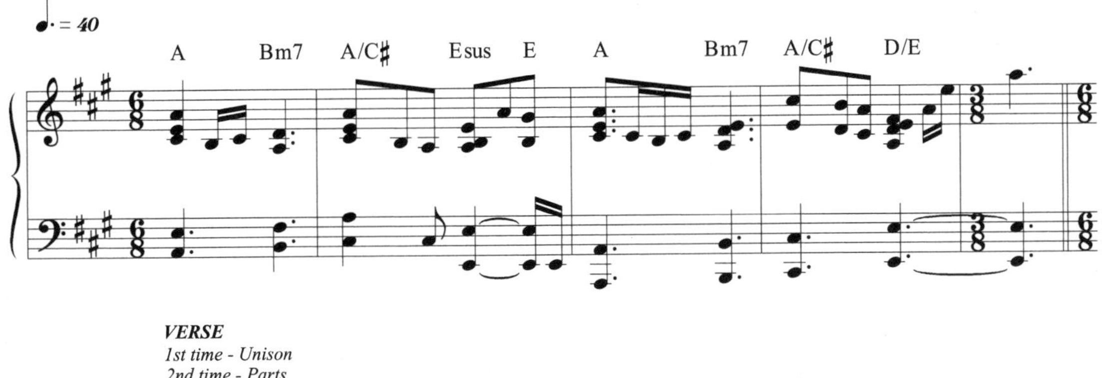

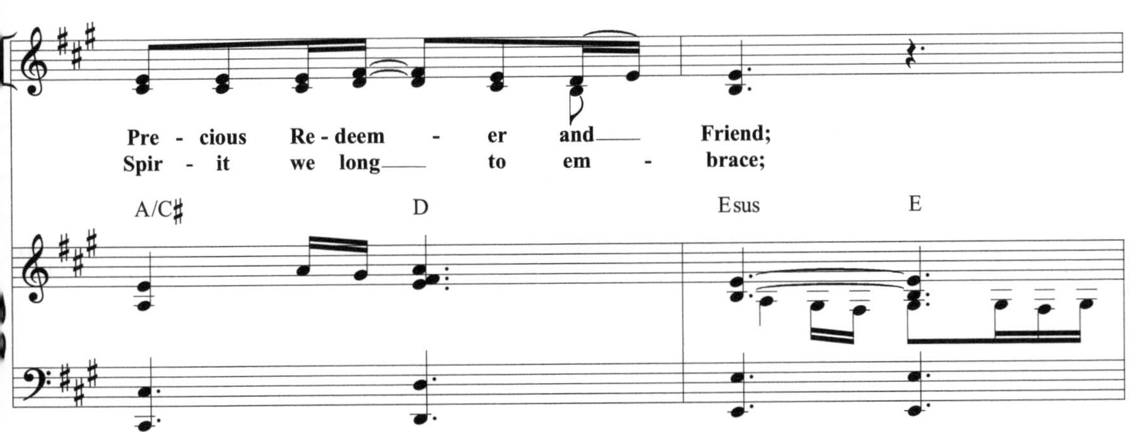

10
Melody - Middle Note
Melody - Bottom Note
Who would - 've thought that a Lamb could
You of - fer hope when our hearts have
F♯m7
F♯m7/E
D
Melody - Top Note
res - cue the souls of men, O, You
hope - less - ly lost the way, O, we've
A
Esus
E♯dim7
F♯m
D
14
1
res - cue the souls of men.
hope - less - ly lost the way.
A/E
Esus
E
F♯m7
D2

CHORUS
Melody - Middle Note
18
2
men.
way.
You are the One that we praise,
A A/G♯ F♯m7 F♯m7/E D E
22
You are the One we a - dore;
You give the heal - ing and
F♯m F♯m7/E D E F♯m F♯m7/E
Melody - Bottom Note
Melody - Top Note
grace our hearts al - ways hun - ger for, O, our
D A Esus E♯dim7 F♯m D
6
29
hearts al-ways hun - ger for.
A/E Esus E A Bm7 A/C♯ D/E B♭ Cm7

31
VERSE
Al-might-y, In-fi-nite Fa - ther,
Bb/D Eb/F Bb Eb/Bb Bb
35
Melody - Middle Note
faith-ful-ly lov-ing Your own; Here in our weak-ness You
Bb/D Eb Fsus F Gm Bb/F
Melody - Bottom Note
Melody - Top Note
find us fal-ling be-fore Your throne, O, we're
Eb Bb Fsus D/F# Gm Eb
39
41
CHORUS
Melody - Middle Note
fal-ling be-fore Your throne. You are the One that we
Bb Fsus F Bb Bb/A Gm Gm7/F

praise, You are the One we a - dore;
E♭ F Gm Gm7/F E♭ F
5
Melody - Bottom Note
You give the heal - ing and grace our hearts al - ways hun - ger
Gm Gm7/F E♭ B♭ Fsus D/F♯
48
Melody - Top Note
1
for, O, our hearts al - ways hun - ger for.
Gm E♭ B♭ B♭/F F B♭ B♭/A
51
2
3
3
O, our
hearts al - ways hun - ger for; Our
B♭/D D E♭ F/E♭ E♭

Medley Options: Show Me Your Ways; Jesus, Name Above All Names.

...You are the one I praise. Jeremiah 17:14 (NIV)

You Are The One

Words and Music by
ALVIN SLAUGHTER

rea - son for liv - ing; You are the One I praise.
Cmaj7
Bm7(♭5)
E7(♯5♯9)
Am7
C/D
G
F6
C
13
CHORUS
You are the One that makes my feet start danc - ing; You are the One that drives the
Praise Team
You are the One;
You are the One;
G7
C9
G7
17
Third time to Coda
dark clouds a-way; You are the One, You're my rea - son for liv - ing;
You are the One;
Am7
C/D
Dm7
F/G
Cmaj7
Bm7(♭5)
E7(♯5♯9)

21
VERSE
You are the One I praise. I praise You for the ver-y breath I breathe,
You are the One I praise.
Am7
C/D
G
G13
G9/B
Cmaj7
Gsus/A
I praise You for sup - ply-ing all my needs, I praise You for a-
Tenors only
Ver-y breath I breathe;
All
All my needs;
G11
Cmaj7
G13
G11
25
maz - ing love, sweet a-maz - ing love, that I've nev - er, nev - er known;
Sweet a-maz - ing love;
Nev-er;
Cmaj9
G2/B
E7(♭9)
E7
Gmaj7/A
A9
C/D

29
I praise You for the joy You've giv - en me
I praise You for in
O,
You give me joy, so much joy;
F/G G13 Cmaj7 Gsus/A G11
33
You I am com - plete,
I give You my heart, my mind, my soul,
I am com-plete;
Cmaj7 G13 G11 Cmaj9 G2/B E7(♭9)
1.
I'm Yours, take con-trol,
take con-trol.
Take con-trol;
Yeah.
E7 Gmaj7/A A9 C/D

D.S. al Coda
2.
take con - trol.
Take con - trol;
Yeah.
A9
C/D
Coda
41
You are the One I praise.
You are the One I praise.
I praise You,
Am7
C/D
G
C/E
F2
Gm7
C7
Praise Team add if desired
Praise;
I praise You, Lord,
I praise You;
Gm7
C7
Gm7
C7
Gm7
C7

Medley options: We've Come To Praise Him; More Than Enough.

...Love him with all your heart, with all your understanding and with all your strength... Mark 12:33 (NIV)

You Are The One I Love

Words and Music by
LENNY LeBLANC

fell a-part, I'm so glad You un - chained me. You
C G D G
17
CHORUS
1st and 2nd times - All
3rd time - Solo
are the One that I love, Light of the world sent
G G/B C D G G/B
20
3rd time - All
from a-bove; Sing hal-le-lu-jah, shout to the Lord; You
C D G B7 Em7
24
last time to Coda
are the One, You are the One, You are the One,
Am7 G/B C D Am7 G/B

28
You are the One I love.
C D G G/B C2 D G G/B D
VERSE 2
Solo
All
Melody - Bottom Note
2. If I knew the song that the an-gels sing, we'd be sing-ing to-
G C G G
Solo
geth-er; I can't wait for e-ter-ni-ty,
D G G C G
All
Soloist - Top Note
prais-in' Your name for-ev-er. You
G D G G G/B C G/D

41
BRIDGE
Solo
Lord, search my heart, and
Em7 G/B C Am G C2 D/F♯
45
find it ev - er true; I pray that my dev - o -
G G/B C2 Am7
49
tion will al - ways be to You. Oh, You
G/B C2 Dsus D
52
Coda
CHORUS
You are the One. You are the One
C D G G/B

56
that I love, Light of the world sent from a-bove; Sing
C D G G/B C D
hal-le-lu-jah, shout to the Lord; You are the One,
G B7 Em7 Am7 G/B
You are the One, You are the One, You are the One, You
C D Am7 G/B C D
are the One, You are the One I love.
64
Am7 G/B C D G G/B C D

Medley Options: Rise Up and Praise Him; Can't Stop Talking.

Both riches and honor come from You, and You reign over all... I Chronicles 29:12 NKJ

You Reign

Words and Music by
MARK CONDON

9
All
Lord, we praise You in maj - es - ty, we
G♭
C♭2/G♭
shout Ho - san - nas to the King of all kings. You
D♭/G♭
C♭2/G♭
G♭
13
CHORUS
reign, You're the Ho - ly One; You
G♭
F♭/G♭
C♭/G♭
reign, be - side You there is none; You
G♭
F♭/G♭
C♭/G♭

17
reign as the Lord of our lives;
Gb
Fb/Gb
Cb/Gb
Lord, You for - ev - er reign;
Abm7
Gb/Bb
Abm/Cb
Gb/Db
Abm/Db
Cb2/Gb
Gb
21
VERSE
Ladies
Glo - ry, glo - ry, it all be - longs to You with
G
C2/G
hal - le - lu - jahs, Lord, we fill this room;
D/G
C2/G

25
All
As Your pres - ence be - gins to en - ter in, we in -
G
C2/G
ten - si - fy our wor - ship and we be - gin to sing. You
D/G
C2/G
G
29
CHORUS
reign, You're the Ho - ly One; You
G
F/G
C/G
reign, be - side You there is none; You
G
F/G
C/G

33
reign as the Lord of our lives;
G
F/G
C/G
Lord, You for - ev - er reign;
You're the
Am7
G/B
Am/C
G/D
Am/D
C2/G
G
37
BRIDGE
Mas - ter of it all, our Sav - ior and our King;
You're the
Gm7
C7
rul - er of our hearts, You're the rea - son why we sing;
All
Gm7
C7

41
Heav'n and earth is Yours, You're the Lord of ev - 'ry-thing;
Gm7
C7
Ev-en the gates of hell shall cry the prais-es that we sing. You're the
Gm9
1.
2.
prais - es that we sing. You
46
CHORUS
reign,
G
F/G
You're the Ho - ly One; You reign, be -
C/G
G
F/G

50
side You there is none; You reign as the
C/G
G
F/G
Lord of our lives; Lord, You for - ev - er
C/G
Am7
G/B
Am/C
G/D
Am/D
54
BRIDGE
reign; You're the Mas - ter of it all, our
C2/G
G
Gm7
Sav - ior and our King; You're the rul - er of our hearts, You're the
C7
Gm7

58
rea - son why we sing; All Heav'n and earth is Yours, You're the
C7
Abm7
Lord of ev - 'ry-thing; Ev-en the gates of hell shall cry the
Db7
Abm9
62
CHORUS
prais - es that we sing. You reign,
Ab
Gb/Ab
You're the Ho - ly One; You reign, be -
Db/Ab
Ab
Gb/Ab

65
side You there is none; You reign as the
Db/Ab
Ab
Gb/Ab
Lord of our lives; Lord, You for - ev - er
Db/Ab
Bbm7
Ab/C
Bbm/Db
Ab/Eb
Bbm/Eb
69
reign; You reign as the
Db2/Ab
Ab
Ab
Gb/Ab
Lord of our lives; Lord, You for - ev - er
Db/Ab
Bbm7
Ab/C
Bbm/Db
Ab/Eb
Bbm/Eb

73
reign; You reign as the
Db2/Ab Ab Ab Gb/Ab
2nd time to Coda
Lord of our lives;
Lord, You for - ev - er
Db/Ab
Bbm7 Ab/C Bbm/Db Ab/Eb Bbm/Eb
77
reign;
Db2/Ab Ab Abm7
Db7 Abm7

D.S. al Coda

rea - son why we sing; All

D♭7

Medley options: Mourning Into Dancing; Celebrate The Lord Of Love.

Because your love is better than life, my lips will glorify you. Psa. 63:3 NIV

Your Love For Me

Words and Music by
DON HARRIS and GARY SADLER

9
earth and sky;
have for me;
Your good-ness fills my life
I'm drink-ing from the cup
G
D
A
11
1st time - Worship Leader only
2nd & 3rd time - All
in ev-'ry cir-cum-stance,
of pure and end-less grace,
My heart is o-pen wide,
G
Em7
G
CHORUS
All
15
My hands are lift-ed high.
You are my God and
Em7
G A
D
I am Your ser-vant,
I am in awe of Your love for me;
Em7
D/F♯
G A

19
Your mer - cy flows though I don't deserve it, I want to shout it out,
D
Em7
D/F♯
last time to Coda
1.
24
I'm in awe of Your love for me.
C
G
A
D
A
25
G
A
D
A
G2
2.
29
Worship Leader
All
awe of Your love for me. I wan - na shout it out, I'm in
G
A
C
Em7

30
Worship Leader
All
awe of Your love for me.
Ooh, yeah; I'm in
G
A
C
Em7
awe of Your love for me.
I'm in awe of Your love for me.
G
A
C
Em7
G
A
Coda
36
CHORUS
37
awe of Your love for me.
You are my God and I am Your ser-vant,
G
A
D
Em7
40
I am in awe of Your love for me;
Your mer - cy flows though
D/F♯
G
A
D

Medley options: Step By Step (O God You Are My God).

For great is your love, reaching to the heavens; your faithfulness reaches to the skies. Psa. 57:10 NIV

Your Love Is Extravagant

Words and Music by
DARRELL EVANS

2nd time - Men
2nd time - All
Ooo,
Mm,
in - ti - mate;
C♯m
B
E/G♯
A2
C♯m
B
13
1st time - Worship Leader
2nd time - All
I find I'm mov - ing to the rhy - thms of Your grace, Your fra - grance
E/G♯
A2
C♯m
B
17
is in - tox - i - cat - ing in our se - cret place;
Your love,
E/G♯
A2
C♯m
B
E/G♯
A2

2nd time - Praise Team
W. L.
Your love, is ex - trav - a - gant.
C♯m
B
E/G♯
A2
C♯m
B
CHORUS
21
All
W. L.
Spread wide in the arms of Christ is the love that cov - ers
B
F♯m7(add4)
E/A
A2
25
All
last time to Coda
sin; No great - er love have I ev - er known,
B
B
F♯m7(add4)

1.
W. L.
You con-sid-ered me a friend,
cap-ture my heart a-gain.
E/A
A2
B
E/A
A2
29
Cap-ture my heart a-gain.
E/G♯
A2
C♯m
B
E/G♯
A2
C♯m
B

33
2.
W. L.
D.S.
You con - sid - ered me a friend,
E/A
A2
B
Coda
W. L.
You con - sid - ered me a friend, cap - ture my heart a - gain.
E/A
A2
B
E/A
A2
37
W.L. & Praise Team ad libs
Sung 1st time only
Cap - ture my heart a - gain.
E/G♯
A2
C♯m
B

Medley options: I Love To Be With You; Rainbow Song.

INDEX A
INDEX ACCORDING TO KEY AND TEMPO

D MAJOR

D MINOR

E MAJOR

E MAJOR

F MAJOR

INDEX B
TOPICAL INDEX

INDEX C
INDEX ACCORDING TO FIRST LINES

INDEX D
INDEX ACCORDING TO SCRIPTURE REFERENCE

INDEX E
INDEX OF COPYRIGHT OWNERS

Alvin Slaughter Music, (adm by Integrity's Hosanna! Music) c/o Integrity Incorporated, 1000 Cody Road, Mobile, AL 36695: Selections 1252, 1262.

Brooklyn Tabernacle Music, c/o Integrated Copyright Group, P.O. Box 24149, Nashville, TN 37202: Selection 1211.

Darlene Zschech/Hillsongs Publishing, (adm in the U.S. and Canada by Integrity's Hosanna! Music) c/o Integrity Music Inc., 1000 Cody Road, Mobile, AL 36695: Selections 1198, 1226.

Dayspring Music, Inc., c/o Word Music, P.O. Box 128469, Nashville, TN 37212-8469: Selections 1211, 1261.

Doulos Publishing, (adm by The Copyright Company, Nashville, TN) c/o The Copyright Company, 40 Music Square East, Nashville, TN 37203: Selection 1239.

EMI Blackwood Music, Inc./Muse-O-Music LLC, All rights on behalf of EMI Blackwood Music, Inc., and Muse-O-Music LLC administered by EMI Blackwood Music, Inc., 810 Seventh Avenue, New York, NY 10019-5818: Selection 1220.

Harvest Fire Music, 2600 South LaBrea, Los Angeles, CA 90016: Selection 1251.

Heart Of The City Music, (adm by Word Music, Inc.) c/o Word Music, Inc., 65 Music Square West, Nashville, TN 37203: Selection 1228.

Hergy Bear Music, P.O. Box 218803, Nashville, TN 37221: Selection 1220.

High Hill Songs, c/o Music Lifeline, PMB# 20, 7005 Avenue U, Brooklyn, NY 11234: Selection 1227.

His Spirit Music, c/o SpiritSound Music Group, 1441 Guthrie Drive NW, Cleveland, TN 37311: Selection 1255.

Integrity's Alleluia! Music, c/o Integrity Music, Inc., 1000 Cody Road, Mobile, AL 36695: Selections 1196, 1200, 1202, 1203, 1208, 1209, 1210, 1213, 1216, 1234, 1236, 1244, 1246, 1258.

Integrity's Hosanna! Music, c/o Integrity Music, Inc., 1000 Cody Road, Mobile, AL 36695: Selections 1195, 1204, 1206, 1207, 1212, 1224, 1225, 1232, 1243, 1245, 1247, 1248, 1249, 1252, 1253, 1254, 1256, 1262, 1263, 1265, 1266.

Integrity's Praise! Music, c/o Integrity Music, Inc., 1000 Cody Road, Mobile, AL 36695: Selections 1197, 1199, 1205, 1207, 1215, 1217, 1219, 1229, 1231, 1233, 1235, 1237, 1238, 1242, 1257, 1264.

LenSongs Publishing, 287 Spout Springs Road, Muscle Shoals, AL 35661: Selections 1195, 1263.

Maranatha Praise, Inc., c/o The Copyright Company, 40 Music Square East, Nashville, TN 37203: Selection 1223.

MDM Publishing, 1984 Cranberry Isles Way, Apopka, FL 32712: Selection 1250.

N-Flyt Music, 152 Twin Oaks Drive, Nashville, TN 37211: Selection 1201.

Rettino/Kerner Publishing, c/o Acuff-Rose Music Publishing, Inc., 65 Music Square West, Nashville, TN 37203: Selection 1230.

Reuben Morgan/Hillsongs Publishing, (adm in the U.S. and Canada by Integrity's Hosanna! Music) c/o Integrity Music Inc., 1000 Cody Road, Mobile, AL 36695: Selections 1222, 1241.

Rocketown Music/Sweater Weather, c/o Rocketown Music, LLC, P.O. Box 967, Franklin, TN 37065: Selection 1240.

Roger Ryan Music, 1437 Timber Valley Drive, Nashville, TN 37214: Selection 1252.

Ron Kenoly Music, c/o Ron Kenoly Music, 8484 Wilshire Blvd., Suite 850, Beverly Hills, CA 90211: Selection 1260.

Russell Fragar/Hillsongs Publishing, (adm in the U.S. and Canada by Integrity's Hosanna! Music) c/o Integrity Music Inc., 1000 Cody Road, Mobile, AL 36695: Selections 1218, 1221.

Scott's Residence Distributors, (adm by Doulos Publishing) c/o The Copyright Company, 40 Music Square East, Nashville, TN 37203: Selection 1239.

Shepherd's Heart Music, Inc., (adm by Dayspring Music, Inc.) P.O. Box 128469, Nashville, TN 37212-8469: Selection 1259.

SwanSound Music Publishing, P.O. Box 1227, Arden, NC 28704: Selection 1214.

Word Music, c/o Word Music, Inc., 65 Music Square West, Nashville, TN 37203: Selections 1228, 1261.